Beyond Theory

Practical Strategies
Making a Difference in Schools

Tyrone Olverson | Dr. Catherine L. Barnes | Scott Taylor

Open Books
PRESS

Bloomington, Indiana

Published by Open Books Press, USA

www.openbookspress.com
An imprint of Pen & Publish, Inc.
Bloomington, Indiana
(812) 837-9226
info@PenandPublish.com
www.PenandPublish.com

Acknowledgments

I want to thank my wonderful wife, Shelly, and children, Tysson and Olivia for their patience. I know you will give this book two thumbs up.

A special thank you to my professional educational thought leaders and mentors: David Baker, Ken Baker, Tim Brown, Steve Dackin, Don Darby, Julie Davis, Ken Dirr, David Distel, Rebecca DuFour, Rick DuFour, Robert "Bob" Eakers, Cassandra Erkins, Nancy Evers, Nancy Gibson, Cathy Hamilton, Shelly Hamler, Stephanie Hirsch, Dan Hoffman, Sherri Houghton, Terrance Hubbard, Jake Hudson, Susan Lang, Daniel Lawler, Randy Leist, Aaron Mackey, Mike Mattos, Michelle Means-Walker, Thomas Moffitt, Michael Mooney, Bobby Moore, Anthony Muhammad, Dennis Peterson, Mari Isom-Phillips, Dan Ross, Richard "Dick" Ross, Bill Sears, Harvey Silver, Jim Smith, Dennis Sparks, Ray Spicher, Thomas Tucker, Philip Wagner, Michael White, Craig Williams, Ken Williams, and Ted Ziegler. A special thank you to these educational giants who are greatly missed and who paved my way on this educational journey: Dr. Ray Bauer, Dr. Lionel Brown, and Dr. Richard Denoyer.

As one reads the book they will see the influences each of you have had on my life and what gifts you have shared with me. Thank you for allowing me to pay forward your collective wisdom to the school systems in which I have been honored to lead, and to the "boys and girls" future leaders will lead.

Every student achieves, no exceptions, and no excuses!

—*Tyrone Olverson*

First and foremost, I would like to thank God for this accomplishment. I also thank my husband for standing beside me throughout this process. He and my darling daughter Teraney have been my inspiration and motivation. Thanks for understanding when I was writing this book instead of hanging out with you and for supporting me without complaining. They have been my rock, and I dedicate this book to them. I'd like to thank my mother, Earlie, Aunt Armerdell, and loving grandmother Martha for allowing me to follow my ambitions, no matter how crazy they seemed. My family has always supported me throughout my career and while authoring this book and I really appreciate it. My siblings, especially Martha and Joe, have always jumped in to make sure I had time to do what I needed to do while Albert, Robert, Trina, Miguel, Marquise, and Gordon pushed me to set an example by demanding nothing but the best from me. You wouldn't allow me to do anything less and I appreciate your confidence in my ability to get this done. To my super supportive friends, Stefanie Walker, Elka Martin-Fleming, Crystal Lewis, Chiquita Rivers, Sheryl Dumont, Sabrina Session-Jones, Yolanda Sanders, Janie and Ellis Anderson, Michelle Willis, Trevor Clayton, and Reggie Peterson; you guys are the best. Without your pushing and making me take a moment to breath, I wouldn't have made it through this process with some semblance of sanity. Special thanks to my mentors, Dr. Alvin G. White, Debra Bass, Mary Brown,

Dr. Sylvia Johnson, Carol Daniels, Pastor Shirley Watts, Dr. Bernard Hamilton, Henry Flenory, E. Pat Warren, Dr. Geneva Sparks, Betty Burney, and Linda Eastman. You all have poured so much into me and have shown me the ropes in education, business, and life. Without your knowledge, encouragement, and tough love I wouldn't have ventured into or continued with my mission when it appeared to be too much to handle. Many of the lessons you have made me learn over the years have ultimately contributed to or enhanced this work. I'd like to especially thank Soror Sheryl Underwood for encouraging me to stay the course and supporting me as a writer as well as Jacqueline Jones, Sanaa Hamilton, Chelvert (CJ) Wellington, and Kendra Thomas-Ward for asking questions and demanding answers. Because of your quest for knowledge I had to stay on a quest of my own. You guys are the iron that keeps me sharp. I would also like to extend a special thank you to Carlene Smith. You were an incredible assistant principal and an amazing instructional leader which was key to our implementation and overall school success. Thank you, Dr. Stephanie James, for trusting me to guide and develop countless leaders through your graduate program. I appreciate you allowing me the freedom to manage my projects and exceed state and local standards. Thank you for requiring me to stay current and using me as a resource which kept me researching and developing to stay on the cutting edge of national and international trends. I'd really like to thank my coauthors for providing me with the opportunity to work with such amazing educators on this book. I appreciate the opportunity to provide my experiences and knowledge to help make this book a reality. I look forward to our next adventure! I owe a huge thanks to Derek and Alayna for providing excellent support and advice as our technical reviewers and project coordinators. All of their efforts helped to make this book complete. We couldn't have done it without you.

—Dr. Catherine L. Barnes

Thank you to my wonderful wife, Becky and my terrific children, Mariel, Emily, Beth and Austin.

Thank you to our editors and advisors: Alayna Gray, Derek Richey, Beth Johnston, Mariel Taylor

Thank you to the most outstanding elementary staff ever! The staff of Crestwood Elementary School!

Thank you to many of my colleagues for their incredible knowledge and talent: Dr. James Sandfort, Dr. Jim Simpson, Dr. Vic Lenz, Dr. Nancy Rathjen, Kathy Bade, Dr. Tara Sparks, Chuck Triplett, Donna Rasnic, Dr. Megan Stryjewski, Dr. Brian McKenney, Dr. Craig Hamby, Suzanne Bright and Mary Hogan.

—Scott Taylor

Table of Contents

Introduction

Let's Get Started!

Congratulations! You have just started to read a book that could change your instructional outcomes, and simplify your way of work. This hands-on resource was created by leaders working in the trenches, who have navigated the road to school improvement. The book outlines procedures and strategies that led to accelerated student achievement in several diverse schools led by three administrators, in three different states. The book shares real-life experiences and provides practical examples, templates and processes proven to change culture and advance overall school performance. The authors share experiences gained in fast-paced school settings, provide an insightful look at the Eight Cylinder Reform Model, offer information on the development and revitalization of the Professional Learning Community (PLC) framework and answer key questions about meeting the academic needs of students while building a school and community culture of high expectations, high accountability, and high student performance. Using this book will help meet the ever-increasing demands on your time and show you simple strategies that will make a vast difference in your personal and professional performance. The following provides an introduction to the Eight Cylinder Reform Model. Additional resources are available and can be found at the authors' website www.beyondtheoryedu.com.

Introduction of the Eight Cylinder Reform Model

Have you ever looked closely at a new initiative or new reform and wondered if it were created by aliens for people living on another planet? Unfortunately, reforms are often designed to meet the needs of a few and only address some of the issues we face in our very complex environments. Schools are flooded with an abundance of initiatives to implement or left without the needed resources to adequately impact overall performance. Fortunately, those of us who work in schools understand that a reform model must do the following: uncover and address academic and non-academic variables, provide a plan for implementation and monitoring progress, be clearly understood by everyone involved, and hold everyone accountable for understanding and actively fulfilling his/her role in the continual improvement plan. The Eight Cylinder Reform Model (ECRM) will do just that.

Frustration frequently breeds innovation. Using the Individual Guided Staff Development (IGSD) model as a guide, Tyrone Olverson and his mentor Jake Hudson developed the ECRM school improvement procedure to simplify, clarify and streamline the school improvement plan. This comprehensive reform model is not a program and should not be layered on top of unproductive academic or social practices. Instead, it is a system that changes culture and impacts performance. At the heart of the ECRM are eight tenets working efficiently in unison to accelerate achievement and change the school's climate and culture for the better. These eight core components, when clearly understood, communicated and collaboratively implemented, allow you to take the first step in building a comprehensive improvement plan.

The eight components are: planning the continual improvement plan, prioritizing curriculum and schedule, scheduling school-wide interventions, developing grade-level intervention plans, creating intervention notebooks, creating a new majority, implementing a year-long plan, and measuring results and celebrating success. Each of these components will be explained in much greater detail as we share our stories, thoughts, research and resources.

Readers will benefit from the diverse leadership styles, educational settings and methods of implementation that the three authors have experienced throughout their careers. This book will provide valuable resources and strategies to fit every scenario you can imagine. This resource offers real life examples, samples of documents and intertwines the realities that let you know that you are not alone in your quest for organizational success. The authors have served as teachers and leaders in elementary, secondary, post-secondary schools and at the district level. They bring both corporate and educational experience to the table to make this resource a must read for current and future educators.

"If you want to go quick, go alone; if you want to go far, go together."

—African Proverb

Abstract

This book focuses on a continual improvement model designed to save leaders time, build a culture of commitment and accountability, and guide the continual improvement plan. It provides practical examples, templates and processes that educators committed to organizational advancement, should use in collaborating with their staff to set and meet recognized goals. The authors present specific examples that clearly illustrate how their schools implemented the different components of the Eight Cylinder Reform Model. They will guide readers through how the components were utilized to improve student achievement, build a sustainable culture of high performance, and create a strong and accountable environment within any classroom, school, community or organization.

The book (and website) offers resources along with examples, samples and best practices that provide a template for jump-starting your reform process. It causes readers to reflect on current realities and practices to determine appropriate goals for their environment. The chapters ahead offer tools school administrators, teachers and business leaders can use to create amazing results. By implementing the process, you gain engaging delivery methods and discover proven strategies that lead to improved student performance. The authors hope this book will simplify and focus the work for administrators and teacher leaders by helping to align efforts within the Professional Learning Community.

Author Biographies

Tyrone Olverson, M.Ed., is currently Superintendent of Finneytown Local School District in Southwestern, Ohio. He was the former curriculum director and principal in the Licking Heights Local School District in central Ohio. While at Licking Heights the district earned an "A" rating for Standards Met, Overall Value-Added, Gifted Value-Added, 4-year Graduation Rate, and 5-year Graduation Rate by the Ohio Department of Education. During his tenure at the high school, the school earned an "Excellent" rating as determined by the Ohio Department of Education by increasing the Performance Index to 104 from 96, and meeting 12 of 12 indicators for the first time ever. Other high school works include the development of a small learning community (SLC) and Freshmen Academy programs of five- and four-person teacher teams. The SLCs and Freshmen Academy implemented Professional Learning Communities at Work™ concepts that demonstrated increased student achievement over consecutive years. During his tenure as a high school administrator, his staff conducted several action research projects that identified the "good, bad, and ugly" in raising student achievement.

His former assignment as principal of Reynoldsburg Junior High School and Waggoner Road Junior High School in Reynoldsburg, Ohio provided him with a strong understanding of the Professional Learning Communities at Work™ concepts. During the 2006–2007 school year, Waggoner Road Junior High School received the Battelle for Kids SOAR Award for raising student achievement among seventh- and eighth-grade students within the top 3.5 percent of the state.

While principal of Lincoln Heights Elementary School in Cincinnati, Ohio, Olverson's school was selected to participate in the National Staff Development Council's "12 under 12" initiative. He believed that 12 years was too long to wait to improve student achievement for the urban school's 400 underprivileged students, which were 99 percent African-American and 100 percent Free Breakfast and Lunch participants. Lincoln Heights was one of four elementary schools across the nation to take on this No Child Left Behind challenge. Through the creation and implementation of a research-based reform (ECRM), student achievement increased each year based on school and state assessment data.

Tyrone credits much of his strong understanding of urban, suburban, and rural education, and which strategies work best to ensure all students achieve academic success over the past 20 plus years to his life experiences in education and to his educational mentors. His diverse experience as an educator include serving as a middle school teacher, an administrator at the elementary, middle, and high school levels and district administrator in urban, urban-suburban, suburban and rural districts. Many of his mentors either have worked with or work at Learning Forward. He was also a former president of the Learning Forward Ohio affiliation (formerly known as Staff Development Council of Ohio).

His presentations and workshops motivate educators. He models strategies that are thoughtful and engage his audiences in a variety of thought-provoking activities. This ability makes him a dynamic and insightful public speaker. His presentations engage educators from Pre-K to 12th grade settings. Participants come away from his presentations with practical solutions to challenges that can be utilized immediately in their district, school, and classroom settings.

Tyrone earned his Bachelor's Degree from The Ohio State University and his Master's Degree in Educational Administration from the University of Cincinnati, where he also completed coursework in the Urban Educational Leadership (UEL) program. He is completing his Educational Administration Doctoral Program through Concordia University Chicago.

Dr. Catherine Barnes is an educational consultant and former principal from Florida with over 20 years of experience. She is credited with conceptualizing and implementing Duval County Public School's first single-gender instructional model and was recognized nationally, after being featured on CNN, for the research and implementation of this model. She and her team successfully transformed an urban middle school serving a 96% African American, 94% free or reduced lunch, and 54% students with disabilities population. The model, along with the instructional strategies and professional development plan incorporated, shifted the school's culture, increased teacher collaboration within Professional Learning Communities and redefined intentional instruction.

Dr. Barnes specializes in the implementation of data based, targeted instructional and leadership practices that lead to increased student achievement, teacher success, resilient leadership team processes and organizational change. Through workshops, conferences and the use of her 1, 3, and 5 year coaching, monitoring, feedback and development (CMFD) cycles she has worked with leadership and instructional teams in Florida, Georgia, Alabama, Tennessee, Kentucky, South Carolina, Louisiana and Ohio with tremendous results. She has also facilitated energetic sessions on "cultural competency" and the impact of equity and inclusion for the University of Florida's Lastinger MODELS project over the past few years. Dr. Barnes is noted as a dynamic school-based, district, state and national trainer on topics such as RtI, AYP, Urban School Leadership, hybrid and flip classroom concepts, building and sustaining effective Professional Learning Communities, the collection and use of relevant data, prioritization of the curriculum, using data to target instructional practices, strategies for struggling students, finding and funding programs for success, and building school culture. She has recently presented at conferences such as the Southern Regional Educational Board (SREB), National High Schools That Work and Middle Schools That Work conference, the National Alliance of Black School Educators Conference, the National Urban Summit, and COSEBOC National Conference and is a highly sought facilitator for schools, districts and professional organizations.

Dr. Barnes received a Bachelor and Masters Degree from the University of Florida, a Masters Degree from Jacksonville University and a Doctoral Degree from Nova Southeastern University. She gained elementary, secondary and post secondary experience while serving as a teacher, literacy liaison and academic coach, Assistant Principal, Vice Principal, Principal, Leadership Program Facilitator, Certified Urban Leadership Mentor and University instructor. Dr. Barnes is a Schultz Center Fellow, a school accreditation specialist and certified chair with the Southern Association of Colleges and Schools serving SACS/CASI for over nine years. She has conducted action research projects over the past three years which have allowed her to travel to China, Spain and Portugal to evaluate schools and systems, and she also is a contributing editor on several national publications.

Scott Taylor, Ed.S., is an educational consultant and former principal of Crestwood Elementary School in the Lindbergh Schools, St. Louis County, Missouri. Under Scott's direction, Crestwood achieved outstanding results on state achievement tests and for nine years in a row, Crestwood has been named to Missouri "Top 10" lists for high achievement.

Crestwood is the only school in Missouri to have a math AYP score of higher then 80% proficient for the last nine years in a row. Crestwood's subgroups scores have also shown excellent growth and have been ranked among the highest in Missouri for eight years in a row. Crestwood's African American, free/reduced, ELL and IEP subgroups perform at a very high level, and in some areas subgroup scores are four to five times the achievement rate of the State of Missouri. On Schooldigger.com, Crestwood's student achievement ranked 6th in 2007–08, 9th in 2008–09, 4th in 2009–10, 8th in 2010–11, 2nd in 2011–12, and 7th in 2012–13 out of more than 1,100 elementary schools in Missouri. In 2009 and 2011, Crestwood was named a Missouri Gold Star School, the highest honor given by the Missouri Department of Elementary and Secondary Education. In 2011, Crestwood received the U.S. Department of Education's "National Blue Ribbon School Award" and was also named a "National School of Character". Crestwood was the only school in the country in 2011 to receive both of these prestigious recognitions.

Scott has presented workshops and had educational articles published at the local, state and national level. He presented at the National Association of Elementary School Principals (NAESP) convention in 2006, 2007 and 2008. In 2010, Scott and Tyrone presented the "Eight Cylinders" at the National Learning Forward conference. In 2012, Scott shared the opening "Keynote" at the National Character Education Conference in Washington, D.C. Scott has presented in 19 states for thousands of educators. In 2013, Scott was named a Peabody Energy "Leader in Education." Additionally, he is a past recipient of the "St. Louis Distinguished Principal of the Year" award and the Fort Zumwalt School District's "Teacher of the Year" award.

Scott was a principal for 16 years with both the Lindbergh Schools and the Orchard Farm School District in St. Charles, Missouri. He received his Bachelor of Music Education degree from Chapman University in Orange, California, his Masters in Educational Administration from University of Missouri–St. Louis, and Specialists in Educational Administration from University of Missouri–Columbia. Scott truly believes that building relationships with students, staff and parents is vital to improved student achievement. Scott and his wife, Becky, are the proud parents of four children and grandparents of two grandsons.

Setting the Stage: A Call to Action

Tyrone's Story: Ride of a Lifetime

Tyrone's journey into school leadership began in May 2003 when he was a principal in an urban elementary school located in Southwestern Ohio.

In spring, 2003, I was serving my school district as the high school assistant principal. One day, my superintendent called me and asked that I take a ride with him. He said I should be ready to meet in 10 minutes outside the high school. As I walked out of my office and toward the front doors of the school, many thoughts were running through my mind: Why does he want to meet with me? Why now? What was the purpose of the ride? Was this the death ride of an administrator? I was concerned as this was the last year of my first administrative contract and no decision had been made about renewals for the upcoming school year.

As the superintendent's blue car pulled around the corner, it seemed to be speeding up. My stomach churned and my palms became sweaty. As I entered the car, he said, "Buckle up, we're going to take a ride. I want you to see something." I made an attempt at light conversation as he began driving southbound on Interstate 75. I wondered what it was that he wanted me to see, but would not share over the telephone.

A few minutes passed, and we exited the highway, entering a community where we both had grown up. He drove to the highest point in this impoverished community, parked and turned the car off.

Tyrone's Long Walk

"Let's take a walk," he said, unlocking the door. We walked about 75 yards, and then he said, "Are you wondering why we came here?"

"Yes, and I hope this is not the death ride!" I replied, with a childish grin on my face.

"Not at all," he said smiling. "This is where your new school will be built."

My first thoughts spoken aloud were, "Is this where the new ninth-grade building will be built?"

"No, this is where the new elementary school is being built," he replied, a huge smile breaking across his face.

So like any good protégé, I asked, "What elementary school are you referring to?"

He replied, "A school by the name you and I attended as kids."

"Is this the school that I will take over in three years?" My thinking behind three years was that it would take that amount of time to design and build the school. This would allow me to open the new building in September 2006.

He replied, "No, I'm talking about next school year, but don't worry. You will be given the administrative support you need to be successful."

As we continued walking through the neighborhood, I became skeptical about the decision. However, I was willing to assist wherever needed in the school system, and, as most administrators would, I accepted the opportunity to lead that was put forth by my superintendent. I never once asked if other administrative positions were an option. In reflection, I should have asked myself at what cost would I be willing to make this move. However, as my two-year contract was expiring, my only thought at the time was "Thank God, I still have a job."

When I was in third grade, I remember telling my cousin James (RIP) and several close friends that one day I would be the principal of our community school. As my ride with the superintendent concluded that day, I remembered my childhood vision and justified this leadership opportunity as a chance to fulfill my dream and make a difference in the lives of students in the neighborhood where I grew up.

Cathy's Parking Lot to Penthouse Experience

It was a Wednesday evening around 6:30 p.m. and I was leaving the urban high school, where I was assigned as Vice Principal, after a very long day. I was the only administrator left on campus so I was carefully moving across the parking lot to try and get home before it was too late. After spending many years in urban schools, I had become accustomed to the late hours and was blindly comfortable coming and going at various times. The families around the schools learn quickly who cares and who is there for their community so they would ensure I had no issues, no matter what time I needed to get there or leave.

I was starting to leave the parking lot when my cell phone rang. I looked at the number for a bit trying to decide if I wanted to hear what was going to be said before I answered. As I picked it up, I was heard saying good night to one of my parents who sat on her front porch nightly watching the grandkids play. She always made a point of saying, "Get on home Ms. Principal, we need you here tomorrow," as I left the school, and tonight was no different. The otherwise refreshing voice of my Regional Superintendent was unsettling because the rumor mill, in the large yet very small district, was so similar to a soap opera that I had been told that I was going to be promoted or moved by the end of the week, and the places I heard I was going offered no change. I think I was shaken because so many changes were being made and although I knew I deserved to be promoted, I also knew the road to promotion often had little to do with hard work or with you "deserving" the advancement.

It was also not uncommon for principals and vice principals to get phone calls late in the afternoon or evening about an issue that was bubbling up, so I didn't know what to expect. It now seems impossible for all of these things to be going on in my mind during that split-second, but they were. Although I felt my Regional Superintendent was a great guy who supported me and my career, I reluctantly said, "Hello."

"Hey Cathy, are you at home yet or are you still at the school?"

"I'm still here. Leaving the parking lot now. Is everything OK?"

He paused and said, "I should have known you were still there. I've been really proud of the way that you work and all that you have done. You've been in some pretty challenging situations and have done well."

Not knowing how to respond or where this was going I said, "Thank you."

My Regional Superintendent has been either my direct supervisor or indirect supervisor for about four years. He had worked with me as an assistant principal and had also used me to support other new leaders as I moved from assistant principal to vice principal, so he had good working knowledge of my background and what things I had been able to accomplish as a teacher and administrator. He was a good fellow in every sense of the word and a great supervisor.

He proceeded by saying, "Well, I need to meet with you tomorrow to discuss something with you."

My first thought was, "Are you serious? You can't expect me to wait until tomorrow with so much turmoil."

I guess that came across like I was taking a dramatic pause. He said, "Don't worry, it is a good thing. How would you like to have new keys?"

I wasn't sure what that meant because those who were being called to be promoted to principal were being called to meet with the Superintendent in his office downtown. I hadn't heard of anyone receiving drive-by promotions so I didn't know what to expect. So many thoughts were running through my mind that I couldn't sleep. Why does he want to meet with me? Why am

I moving now? Where am I moving and what new challenges have "they" determined I could handle? The one thing I did know was that the comment new keys couldn't mean promotion because they don't promote people like this.

The next morning came so slowly. I was called to the office when he arrived with the news. "Cathy, let's go for a ride. I want to show you something." I didn't know where we were going but I quickly prepared to leave.

As I was gathering my things, his phone rang. Thank God! It bought me some time to calm the butterflies in my stomach. He ended his call and told me that he had to leave soon so the ride wouldn't be possible. I cringed, thinking, "So, what is it?"

He said, "You are ready to be a principal, and guess what? You will be next year." I looked up and stared at him as if to say, "Huh?" He laughed and said, "Congratulations, you are being promoted to principal, but . . ."

Everything that came after that "but" seemed like a clip from Charlie Brown's classroom—"wha-wha, wha-wha." I was so lost in the mental celebration and praise for getting a principalship. I had no idea what was in store for me from that moment on. He pulled me back by calling my name and asking if I was going to say anything. He knew that I was a very upbeat and jovial person so he probably expected me to break out in song and dance, but I was floored by the great news. I had no idea what reward my hard work had earned me.

My Regional Superintendent sat down in the chair and then he said, "Now listen, I am putting you in the toughest middle school in this district. I know that seems strange but I have watched you work for years and you can handle it." I noticed that he hadn't given me the school's name, yet he continued to share the challenges. He explained that the principal who was there at the time was retiring after being there for one year and that the superintendent wanted the school cleaned up and cleaned up fast. Some of the stories he shared made me wonder if I was being punished or blessed, but I never stopped smiling. I was thrilled that he had so much confidence in me but scared to death about what I was walking into.

After getting the academic, demographic, cultural and community information, I asked which school I had been assigned. He smiled and said, "I was going to take you by there but I just got called back to the office. I don't want you to worry so I'll tell you. You have been assigned to XYZ Middle School. You will do fine there. It is very similar to the schools you have been in so don't worry." How could I not worry? He had just told me the school had declining enrollment in their magnet programs, the feeder schools were beginning to struggle, the discipline was so bad that they were considering getting additional security and police presence, scores were beginning to decline rapidly in the growing targeted subgroups, and we were now serving more students with disabilities, students in poverty, and the teachers were restless, afraid and many were not providing quality instruction. I needed to get my hands on their data to start identifying red flag issues immediately, start looking around for resources and people available to join the team, and call my mother, grandmother and aunt and have them start praying! My mentor, Dr. Alvin G. White's words immediately came to my mind as I entered the building for the first time. Dr. White would always say to me, "Cathy, the higher you climb, the better you see." He couldn't have been more right. What I would see over the next several years was astonishing. Despite all of the good work I had done before this assignment and all of my many experiences, nothing could have prepared me for the road ahead.

Scott's Short Drive

"The purpose of leadership is the improvement of instructional practice and performance."
—Richard Elmore

On August 16, 2004, at 8:15 a.m., I received a phone call while sitting in my office at Crestwood Elementary School. As I turned to answer the phone, my caller ID indicated that my district's superintendent was on the line.

"Scott, do you have a minute?" he asked.

"Sure I do!" I replied.

"Come on over. We need to talk!" my superintendent said.

The three and a half mile drive to central office seemed especially short on this hot summer morning. I anticipated what the topic of our conservation would be—a significant drop in our third grade communication arts score. Our third grade score had declined from 55.1% of our students scoring proficient/advanced in 2003 to 34.5% of students scoring in these top two levels in 2004. I knew the meeting was going to be difficult, but I was totally unprepared for what came next. I was just beginning my third year at Crestwood and our school was still in the early stages of creating a culture that would support ongoing high achievement by our students.

Obviously, superintendents are held extremely accountable for student achievement by their Boards of Education and thus my superintendent was doing his job by holding me accountable for our scores at Crestwood. **Test scores matter. They tell us precisely what we need to know if we have any hope of reforming education and closing the racial gap in academic achievement**" (Thernstrom & Thernstrom, 2003, p. 4). I hold my former superintendent in very high regard and I became a much better administrator due to his excellent leadership— but I must admit that this was a very uncomfortable and unsettling meeting for me. When I walked out, my spirits were low, but I was motivated to do a better job. I wanted to show my superintendent and our Board of Education that Crestwood could be a high-performing school.

During the meeting I was asked to evaluate Crestwood's performance in communication arts (CA). I shared with my superintendent that during the past school year I had predicted a low score in CA. The third grade teachers and I had met twice a month during the 2003-04 school year to discuss our concerns with the achievement level with this group of students. The number "30%" seemed to be the common denominator. More than 30% of the third graders were new to our school, more than 30% came from poverty, more than 30% were African-American, and more than 30% were English Language Learners (ELL). I explained to my superintendent that many of these students had very low academic skills. "**It takes total staff commitment to succeed in the thorny work of reaching low-achieving and underserved students**" (Blankstein, 2004, p. 100). I shared one success story about an African-American student with whom the staff had worked very hard. We predicted that his achievement score would be "Unsatisfactory"; however, he made it to the "Nearing Proficient" level, two levels above the unsatisfactory designation. We were very proud of this student's progress, and I shared other successes with my superintendent, but he was not satisfied.

My superintendent commented that "Nearing Proficient" was not our goal. Students needed to perform at the "Proficient" or "Advanced" level for us to meet state expectations. During the 2003–04 school year, our staff administered monthly self-created common assessments to ensure that our students were making progress. Throughout the year, we realized that we were working with a very low-performing group of students. One of the advantages, and disadvantages, that smaller schools have (our enrollment fluctuated between 300 and 330 students) is that each child's score becomes increasingly important with smaller grade levels and smaller schools. That year, in third grade, we had fewer than 40 students, so each student's score was worth about 2.5 percentage points.

One of the questions my superintendent asked was, "What could your teachers have done better?"

What did our teachers do wrong? The answer was nothing! Our teachers created excellent lesson plans and fostered positive cultures of success in their classrooms. They created common assessments for our students and remained focused on improving student attendance. I was very proud of the efforts of our faculty at Crestwood. Was that enough? This was a very important moment in my career. This conversation with my superintendent motivated me to start using the Eight Cylinder Reform Model and put it into gear. In each of the next nine years to come, Crestwood was named a Missouri Top Ten School and received the ultimate honor being named a "National Blue Ribbon School" in 2011.

Putting the Cylinders into Gear

During the following chapters, we will share how we used each of the components of the Eight Cylinder Reform Model to improve the culture and instructional process at our schools, and how we facilitated the implementation in schools we support. We will share our real-life experiences to help you frame your improvement plan by offering tips, strategies and other insights that focus the mission, align the work, build capacity and smooth the leadership and implementation process during each of the phases of transformation.

Throughout the course of this book, we will be sharing many strategies and interventions to help all students achieve at a higher level. However, remember the message in the following quote as you work with the students in your schools. We need to do more with our students than teach them how to read and write. We need to teach them to be hard workers and good citizens.

"Dear Teacher, I am the survivor of a concentration camp. My eyes saw what no man should witness: gas chambers built by learned engineers, children poisoned by educated physicians, infants killed by trained nurses, and women and babies shot and burned by high school graduates. So I am suspicious of education. My request is: help your students to become more human. Your efforts must never produce learned monsters, skilled psychopaths, educated Eichmann's. Reading, writing and arithmetic are important only if they serve to make our children more human."

—Haim Ginott

Cylinder 1: Developing and Adopting a Building Level Continual Improvement Plan

"Socrates didn't have an overhead projector. He asked questions that bothered people and 3,500 years later people are still talking about him."

—Hanoch McCarty

Schools and their leaders are inundated with data. When planning for school improvement, data overload often occurs making the task of data analysis overwhelming. It is possible to have too much data when planning for school improvement, especially if the data is no longer relevant, redundant or does not point to indicators of change. Relevant, real-time data must be collected, analyzed and utilized in determining:

- **where you are (your current reality);**
- **where you want to go (measurable goals and expected outcomes); and**
- **discrepancies between where you are and where you want to go (gap analysis).**

The Continual Improvement Plan

A Continual Improvement Plan (CIP) is a school-based plan of attack that provides focus to a specific task(s). In providing this focus, team members use available data to design a plan of attack in remedying student and/or academic concerns and challenges.

A CIP is the cornerstone of school improvement and the careful development of this plan is a key component to sustainable continual improvement. The CIP assists a school in addressing various relevant site-based needs and determining targeted improvement processes based on building-specific indicators. The CIP becomes a roadmap to improvement and establishes a set of practices that are aligned, communicated, shared, adopted, expected, implemented, monitored, measured and celebrated regularly. The CIP provides a systematic process for overcoming the challenge of aligning state, district and school-based priorities. It is public and drives every decision made in a school.

Schools show significant progress in improving student performance and school effectiveness when they ensure that plans for continual improvement are school-based, data driven, aligned with the vision and purpose of the school and provide clear expectations for both adult and student behavior. Consistency is also an important driving factor in student learning. The process of developing a CIP is often not as hectic as implementating and embedding the changes into the school culture. When a school fully implements an ongoing and collaborative process for improvement, aligning school practices with expectations for advances in student learning efforts become systematic, sustainable and fully entrenched.

A targeted CIP should:

- provide a current description of student and staff performance;
- outline specific goals for each performance indicator used to determine performance;
- identify who is responsible for data-based revisions, and the associated timelines;
- outline steps and strategies for obtaining desired outcomes;
- describe how and when assessments will occur, and when data is collected and used;
- allow ample time for planning and providing relevant feedback to teachers and students based on both formal and informal results and observations;
- provide targeted professional development for school personnel to address concerns immediately, and to help implement improvement intervention;
- communicate the results of improvement efforts to stakeholders in a timely manner;
- evaluate the effectiveness of each intervention and respond accordingly; and
- identify means to recognize and act upon ineffective service processes or strategies in order to minimize the impact of poor adult performance outcomes.

After this targeted analysis, you are ready to start building your CIP. There are many different templates that exist for CIPs; the following three figures provide a good representation of the formatting that can be used.

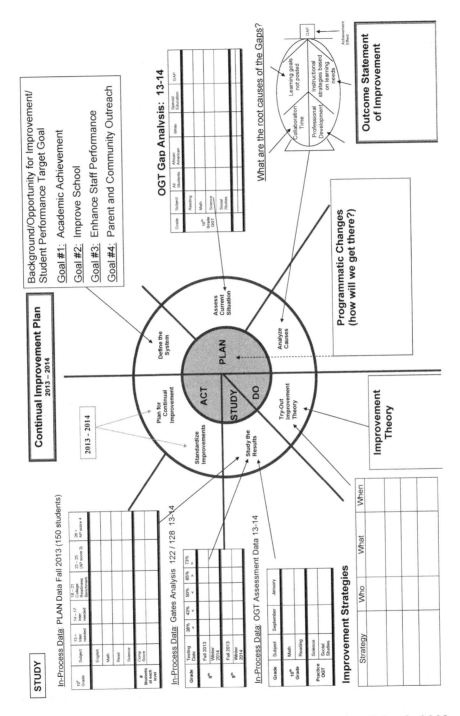

Figure 1: Sample High School CIP provided by Reynoldsburg City Schools 2008

Goal 1.   (Academic)

Create and administer a comprehensive needs assessment process which: reviews data relevant to achievement, discipline, and attendance including parental input. District CIP Correlation: #1, #2, and #5. Title I—#1

Implementation Strategies:

1. Utilize data to update yearly the building CIP. Title I—#1 The assessment instrument being utilized to assess our needs will be the DRA. Other data such as the KRAL, DIBELS, Ohio Proficiency and Achievement Test will be used as a source of data collection to determine which students will receive services. Data will be disaggregated to determine student ability. Students will be grouped in multiple levels.
2. Disaggregate data by sub groups i.e. race, gender, socio-economic, LEP, and disability. Title I—#2
3. Utilize data to determine and prioritize building needs.
4. Create locally developed benchmarks as a basis for measurement. Title I—#4

Evaluation Strategy:

1. A copy of needs assessment instruments will be on file and services will be prioritized and provided based on the summary and analysis of the data collected.
2. During the Fall of the 2004–2005 school year, 3rd grade students scored 23% on the State Reading Achievement Test. We will improve all specific grade-level benchmarks by 20% during the 2005–2006 school year.
3. By the end of the year, 75% of all students assessed by the DRA will achieve their specific grade-level DRA benchmarks.
4. Services to students will be prioritized and provided based on the summary and analysis of the data collected.

System Support: Administration, Reading Specialists, Title I Staff and Teachers.

Notes:

1. The DRA will provide long-term professional growth. Title I students identified through DRA cut scores at each grade level.
2. Reading / Language Arts—20 Minutes a day; Math—90 Minutes a day. At least 65% of the students are below grade level in reading at the beginning of the 3rd grade.
3. Pledge to take place in homerooms and led by the teacher.
4. Students will be in class by 8:30AM.
5. Four ½ day trainings (staff development). Staff will work on skills-based assessments. August 18th — 3-hour staff development w/ Lisa Carter.

Trends: Students enter school a year behind and gradually make progress toward the grade-level outcomes/standards/objectives. The goal is to have students on grade level by the end of 3rd grade by differentiating instruction and providing intervention.

Figure 2: Sample Elementary CIP

Problem	Data Source	Measurable Goals	Performance Measures	Strategies	Timeline
Students are performing poorly on constructed response questions.	-Ohio Achievement Test Results, Spring 2006 -Common Assessments (Spring Exit Exams)	-Improve scores on constructed response items on all Ohio Achievement Tests. -Monitor the progress of all students with their achievement of successfully responding to constructed response items through the common quarterly assessments.	-Ohio Achievement Test Results, Spring 2007 -Pre-Assessments in Reading and Math -Common quarterly assessments	-Provide and critique models of various constructed response items. -Establish the same writing frameworks for all subjects. -Utilize skeletons and outlines for written responses.	Ongoing
Formative assessments are not consistently used to guide daily instruction.	-Classroom Observations -Team Notebooks	Create, share, and utilize formative assessments to make immediate instructional choices for students.	-Data collected from on-going classroom observations -Survey -Quarterly common assessments	-Survey the staff about their knowledge and usage of formative assessments. -Utilize the 5 x 10 model of the "Thoughtful Classroom" observing teachers on a daily basis. -Utilize professional learning teams to share and create formative assessments.	Ongoing

Figure 3: Sample Junior High CIP

Instructional Leadership and the CIP Process

The term instructional leadership has become a catch-all phrase for the ever-changing tasks assigned to school leaders. In its simplest form, it must develop leaders who understand and identify the differences between good and poor instruction, while driving others to optimal performance. Leaders must be able to schedule their time appropriately so that they can monitor instruction, provide timely feedback, partake in learning community practices, serve as a resource, facilitate professional development, oversee the collection of data and support the implementation of the continual improvement plan.

Districts that experience the highest level of success designate school-based leadership positions to provide ongoing support for either the disciplinary or instructional responsibilities of school administrators. These coaches, deans, or in some cases lead teachers, help to set the stage for improvement by ensuring heads of schools are not unable to perform instructional duties because of distractions. Schools without this personnel structure must remain focused on support in the classrooms. The primary goal is to ensure teachers are teaching, and students are learning.

Leaders must stay engaged in the work and remain active in the collection and review of data. The key characteristics of leaders who thrive in a modern learning environment are time-management expertise, commitment to the team, dedication to the work and devotion to school-wide achievement.

The Role of a PLC in the CIP Process

We typically think of a PLC as a group of educators who collaborate to identify best practices and instructional strategies that will increase academic achievement for all students. To ensure that the PLC is positively impacting and informing instruction, and identifying and supporting the goals of the CIP, teachers and leaders should ask the following questions:

- What am I teaching?
- Why am I teaching it?
- How will I know when it is learned?
- When and how will I assess student learning?
- What common assignments and assessments are used to measure growth and compare results?
- How can I simultaneously support the growth of those who already know it and those who do not yet understand?
- How can our team respond to teacher limitations?
- How will I know when we have met our goals?

Getting Buy-In and the Word Out

Once the collection and analysis of data is complete and people as well as processes have been objectively reviewed, it is time to develop a plan to respond. Responses to data must be applied immediately and responsibly in order to address your findings; this may be difficult for those who cannot share in and delegate responsibility. This work cannot be done in isolation, and it is important to involve those who understand the why and the how of all new or revised initiatives.

It is imperative that staff play an active role in evaluating processes, developing new procedures and determining the implementation methods to best meet the established goals. Leaders must encourage and empower others to push the work forward, and not be afraid to share the responsibilities of leadership. This will allow staff to become advocates for the cause and serve as ambassadors for the execution of the CIP.

Schools and students alike must be saturated with simplified reminders of the current reality, targeted goals, individual tasks, performance indicators and path to transition from where they are to where they must be. Much of this information can be communicated via newsletters to staff and students, email blasts, website updates, school announcements or visual representations such as banners and/or flyers. *Become creative in your establishment of effective communication.*

Cathy's Commentary: Conduct an Existing Program Assessment

We must start the improvement plan by looking in the mirror and seeing what is really there. Colleague, close friend and elementary school principal, Crystal Lewis, coined the phrase "kitty cat to lion syndrome" for when one operates in an unrealistic reality by incorrectly perceiving such a reflection. In a much simpler fashion, we have to see ourselves for who we are if we truly want to plan for improvement. During this stage, a school-based leader should complete a comprehensive assessment of relevant, real-time academic and non-academic data. It is equally important to evaluate one's toolbox to ensure the availability and use of best practices. This is not to suggest that you will not have to evaluate and make changes based on individual performance and reassign responsibilities, as data-driven shifts are a huge part of this process. These should be seen as a result of analysis, not the purpose for it.

After reviewing data, leaders must begin conducting a needs-assessment. Academic data could include state testing scores, teacher formal and informal assessments, student work, retention and graduation rates, and teacher grade analysis. Non-academic data could include attendance rates, discipline statistics, culture of the learning environment, student demographics, institutional practices and traditional processes.

During this stage it is important to reflect on the staff. You must determine if you have the right people in the right places, doing the right work. From the clerical staff charged with setting the guest relationship tone to those regularly interacting with students, the CIP must be implemented with fidelity. All staff must be evaluated accurately based on their own data. While your team may believe they are doing a great job, it must be validated with data to ensure decisions are fair and in the best interest of the students.

Building leaders need support to ensure that the entire organization backs the improvement initiatives. In order to get an accurate assessment of the workforce and other high impact factors, leaders must assess the following:

- culture of the teaching and learning environment, referred to by educational consultant, Butch Martin, as cultural complacency. This includes attitude, apathy and institutional practices that perpetuate unproductive behaviors in staff and students;
- effective use of technology;
- relationship between instructional practices and student demographics;
- degree of staff collaboration;
- prioritization of curriculum;
- quality of teaching and learning time;
- accountability measures including goals and expectations;
- support services and available resources;
- alignment of organization-wide processes and procedures; and
- data trends over recent years.

Cylinder 2: Prioritizing the Curriculum and Scheduling

"Don't be a time manager, be a priority manager. Cut your major goals into bite-sized pieces. Each small priority or requirement on the way to your ultimate goal became a mini goal in itself."

—Denis Waitley

With so many mandates and levels of accountability, how do teachers know what to teach, and how do school leaders structure the school day so that it maximizes opportunities for student learning? Many districts have started to utilize pacing guides, learning schedules or other outlines for timing when information is presented to students, and how long it should take. The problem with many of these schedules is that they are developed too late for teachers to appropriately plan, they do not allow much flexibility that limits a teacher's ability to respond to the students he/she serves, and they are not always based on the correct information.

It is not uncommon to find instances, especially in lower performing schools, where teachers operate in survival-mode, using the textbook alone to determine what students should know. This is even more common in environments where district level or external evaluators develop or mandate "cookie cutter" learning cycles with little or no knowledge of the academic environment. Without specific information relative to what students need, it is easy to find classes drifting to either the familiar, the lesson most enjoyed by the teacher, or random selection of content based on materials in the classroom. Setting instructional priorities helps to narrow the focus and ensures teachers are teaching what the students in front of them actually need.

When you pay attention to too many things, you end up paying attention to nothing. This is why it is imperative that we keep our eye on the target and those things that will actually ensure we get there. When we sct instructional priorities using the right information, we ensure that we are paying attention to what matters most in improving academic performance.

When determining instructional priorities teachers must clearly determine:

- What is *essential* for our students to know/learn and what requisite concepts must be taught or reviewed to ensure the new material is learned?
- What is *important* for our students to know or be able to do? How will students need to demonstrate mastery of the concept?
- What is *nice* for our students to know/learn?
- How will we know that students have learned the content?
- What is done differently for students who already know it and those who do not yet understand?

With so many areas of focus in educating students, one must examine and determine where to begin. In prioritizing the curriculum, school leaders and teachers review their curriculum and student assessment data to decide where to focus their energy. In this process, staff members determine which areas of curricular focus will provide the biggest impact for their efforts on improving student outcomes.

How Prioritizing the Curriculum and Scheduling Works

Prioritizing the curriculum and scheduling instructional processes that align with established priorities is critical in improving organizational outcomes. Curriculum-based priorities demonstrate what is most important in bringing about desired outcomes and is an essential aspect of your school improvement plan. A prioritized curriculum provides a focus and direction guiding what is taught when. This should be based on data sets, standards and assessment item specifications.

When school leaders begin the prioritization process, there is certain data needed to set an instructional focus. Teachers and school leaders should look closely at what students should know and should be able to do based on grade and content standards. This information must be aligned with the item specifications for "end of course", district, state and national assessments. Although many would say this leads to "teaching to the test", it is important to face the reality of performance-based employment factors found in value added evaluation systems and other grading or rating systems that make student performance on these assessments an indicator of student, teacher, and school success. Item specifications should provide insight into which benchmarks are considered most important or most highly weighted by those setting district or state performance targets. Those benchmarks with the highest frequency over time should receive the greatest priority in terms of instruction and remediation efforts.

A secondary Language Arts classroom utilized the following focus calendar to help prioritize the curriculum for their students during a particular month.

Oct.	Instructional Focus (IF) & Word of the Week (WW)	Teacher Activity	Teacher Activity	Teacher Activity	Teacher Activity	Teacher Activity
Week 1	IF—Main Idea WW—**Summarize**	Common 5 question formative	Teach concept	Review & walk through	Student practice & reteach	Common 5 question summative
Week 2	IF—Cause & Effect 6th Validity of Info 7th Fact & Opinion 8th WW—**Analyze**	Common 5 question formative	Teach concept	Review & walk through	Student practice & reteach	Common 5 question summative
Week 3	IF—Facts and Opinions WW—**Predict**	Common 5 question formative	Teach concept	Review & walk through	Student practice & reteach	Common 5 question summative
Week 4	IF—Organizational Patterns WW—**Infer**	Common 5 question formative	Teach concept	Review & walk through	Student practice & reteach	Common 5 question summative
Week 5	IF—Context Clues WW—**Describe**	Common 5 question formative	Teach concept	Review & walk through	Student practice & reteach	Common 5 question summative

Figure 4: Secondary Focus Calendar

The Role of Formative and Summative Assessments in Prioritizing Curriculum

Formative assessment data is important to review when prioritizing the curriculum and establishing instructional delivery targets. Formative assessments are key determinants toward future teaching needs and how much time should be dedicated to these topics. Formative assessments do not have to be overly complicated, but should be long enough to give the teacher an indicator of where students are on a particular concept, benchmark or standard. Data collected during a short formative assessment can be used to establish flexible groups for remediation or enrichment activities, to determine what requisite knowledge must be included to ensure mastery of the new content, and to determine how much time should be allotted to the delivery of any content-related material.

It is important to note there is no way to determine, without assessing your students' current readiness and performance level, how much time is needed for students to master a concept. The use of formative assessment data keeps teachers from wasting time on things students already know leaving more time for deeper exploration of more difficult concepts or remediation of basic skills that hinder the learning of new standards.

Formative assessments allow teachers to monitor student learning while receiving ongoing feedback about student strengths and weaknesses, commonly held misunderstandings, and to identify concepts or skills that need remediation immediately. There are numerous examples of formative assessments but one that is gaining popularity is the Exit Ticket (Figures 5 and 6). Exit Tickets can be preprinted for students based on the lesson objectives. Teachers may post a problem, pose a question for student response or have students simply respond to a prompt at the end of each lesson. They are used to revamp instruction and adjust instruction to facilitate the level of mastery identified. There are various exit formats and teachers should choose what works best for them. Two samples are provided to show how they can be used to determine student mastery.

Exit Ticket to Assess Competence and Understanding of Concepts

In the example below, students are asked a question about a concept and are allowed to provide a quick answer to demonstrate their understanding. The question may either be written prior to or provided during class.

EXIT TICKET
Question: Today we discussed the Industrial Revolution. Please list 2 events that served as a catalyst and explain how they helped start this historical period.
Student Response:

Figure 5: Sample Social Studies Exit Ticket

Exit Ticket to Assess Confidence, Independent Thinking, and Evidence

Used for measuring student confidence and determining where students get lost in the process of problem solving. In the example below, students assess their confidence level and respond to questions in the corresponding column to demonstrate their level of understanding.

1) *When answering the question I was:* Choose A, B, or C	**Very Confident** **A**	**Struggled but Got It** **B**	**Had No Clue— Please Help** **C**
2) *Student Feedback:* Respond to the questions *Student can write a note or pose a question to the teacher here*	I knew I had it when . . .	I was doing fine until . . .	I got lost when . . .
3) *Teacher Feedback:*	Celebrate and Show Off $3x+27+12x+14x$	Try Another One $13x + 7 + 6=$	Sit with me in small group or I will come to you

Figure 6: Sample Mathematics Exit Ticket

Summative assessments are used to evaluate student learning at the end of an instructional unit, semester or year. These assessments measure students against an established benchmark or standard. Often these are seen as a unit test, midterm exam, research project or standardized test. Summative assessments help teachers and school leaders identify what content students have mastered. They help teachers determine what material needs to be revisited and outlines next steps for student improvement. A cycle of formative and summative assessments should be used to set instructional goals and measure progress towards meeting learning targets.

Using the research of Grant Wiggins (2005), the following seven strategies were incorporated into instructional practice to help students understand the learning goals and to support them through the assessment cycles:

1. Provide clear, specific and measurable learning goals to students stating what we want them to learn.
2. Provide samples/models (both good and poor).
3. Provide continual access to descriptive feedback.
4. Provide an avenue for self-assessment.
5. Build instruction around one facet of quality at a time.
6. Focus revision.
7. Self reflect.

How to Optimize Instructional Time

Another important aspect of prioritizing for results is establishing how classroom instructional time is scheduled, valued and utilized. Many schools, districts and states mandate an instructional structure based on various models designed to ensure bell-to-bell instruction occurs daily. Although many of these structures are in place, they do not always guarantee learning is continual and teachers are best utilizing their instructional time. Teachers are the key to making instructional time rewarding for students and moving students forward within the time scheduled. Leaders must create a sense of urgency, foster a culture of commitment, and monitor instructional processes consistently to ensure there is no free time during the instructional day. Leaders must monitor what they value because what gets monitored gets done. This is the same for teachers as well. Students know what their teachers feel is most important based on what they collect, assess, provide corrective instead of summative feedback on, and what they monitor and track.

Figures 7, 8 and 9 provide samples of prioritized school-wide and classroom instructional formats designed to incorporate remediation while allowing teachers to continue with introducing new content. These models have helped teachers structure the delivery of material and give students a process that fosters a culture of learning.

Elementary Sample School-Wide Prioritized Curriculum Schedule

8:45–11:30 a.m.	Literacy Block: Reading, Writing, Spelling
11:30–12:00 p.m.	Lunch
12:00–1:00 p.m.	Math
1:00–1:40 p.m.	Social Studies
1:40–2:00 p.m.	Recess
2:05–2:45 p.m.	Science
2:50–3:20 p.m.	Special Classes (art, music, physical education and technology)

Figure 7: Elementary School-Wide Schedule

Secondary Sample Prioritized Classroom Schedule—45-minute block

Warm Up and Focus Lesson: Data-driven remediation problem based on current assessment data—may or may not be tied to the current lesson	**5 min**
Mini-Lesson with Modeling: Introduce new concept and walk students through the steps of the concept ("I do")	**10 min**
Student Work Period: Guided Practice ("We do") and Independent Practice ("You do")	**20 min**
Closing: Summarize and assessment of understanding	**10 min**

Figure 8: Secondary 45-Minute Block Schedule

Secondary Sample Prioritized Classroom Schedule—90-minute block

Warm Up and Focus Lesson: Data-driven remediation problem based on current assessment data—may or may not be tied to the current lesson	**10–15 min**
Mini-Lesson with Modeling: Introduce new concept and walk students through the steps of the concept ("I do")	**15–20 min**
Student Work Period: Guided Practice ("We do") and Independent Practice ("You do") RtI and small-group instruction takes place while students work in groups or independently on current concepts or enrichment activities	**30–40 min**
Closing: Summarize and assessment of understanding	**10–15 min**

Figure 9: Secondary 90-Minute Block Schedule

Ty's Take: The Prioritization and Implementation Process at Work

We started our process by asking the critical question *"How should a school go about prioritizing the curriculum to impact student performance?"* We examined our school's data to determine what areas of the curriculum needed further focus, taking staff input into consideration throughout the process. We looked at the concepts and processes students needed to master in order to meet performance expectations and show greater success, being sure to look closely at what background or requisite concepts were underneath the benchmark or standard.

Establishing underlying or connected concepts and critical vocabulary were instrumental in moving the school forward. Unfortunately, it is a step often missed in the prioritization and implementation process. We had to stop spending time blaming teachers and students for what our kids did not know and find a way to incorporate needed information in our instructional process. When prioritizing, understanding what, how and when to teach is critical.

We then moved into a process of determining what to do with the time we have with students. Many teachers struggled with extended school-day activities such as homework or outside projects, especially with lower performing students. This made maximizing classroom time critical. We examined our schedule and removed all of the things that interrupted or infringed on instructional time. A colleague suggested that we limit all announcements to a morning news program, except in emergency situations. Another method suggested involved using classroom ambassadors to deliver any non-emergency teacher messages to mailboxes outside of the classroom door to be checked at the end of the period.

We continued to ask, *"What more can classroom teachers do to improve student achievement?"* and *"What can teachers do less of to keep the focus on learning and improving student and teacher success?"* As a result of this questioning, our teachers began to focus on these questions when they encountered new content to teach or when reviewing assessment results. The teachers then were able to better understand what students should know and be able to do and subsequently align instruction to specific grade-level academic content standards. While talking with teachers throughout the year I found that the most beneficial use of teacher time had been geared toward teaching academic content standards and vocabulary.

Most schools face challenges relating to the prioritization of curriculum and scheduling. Our school was no different as our systematic direction was unclear. We had multiple non-connected program offerings. Of the 53 programs offered at our school, 13 had an author or individual who took responsibility and/or credit for the specific program(s) being implemented, and six were achievement and/or academically focused. We had a high staff-to-pupil ratio and we were consistently inconsistent!

We recognized through trial and error that teachers who taught the academic content standards **and** vocabulary in the same building with the same group of students, produced remarkably superior results. After periodic review of our data, we found that students whose teachers actively participated in PLCs and successfully implemented this process with fidelity, outperformed their counterparts by a significant degree.

These teachers were focusing their content, assessing student learning, aligning instruction to real-time data, collaborating to improve their instructional skills and sharing results with students to set new performance goals. Shifts in instruction were also based on assessments, exams and observations. These changes in teacher practices were further validated when I was having a conversation with Rick DuFour (2004) in which he stated, **"Teachers, who engaged and collaborated as a PLC, investigated research-based instructional strategies to promote greater depth of knowledge and learning."**

Writing SMART Goals to Maintain Focus

We determined that those seeking to accelerate student learning would need to do a few things well while focusing on results. At our school, the teachers were asked to establish SMART goals to illustrate their focus. This was an integral component in developing and adopting our building and grade-level improvement plans. SMART goals are:
   (S)mart
   (M)easurable
   (A)ttainable
   (R)ealistic
   (T)imely

SMART goals are very clear and straightforward, as can be seen in the examples below.

- Elementary: By the end of the week, 95% of my third-grade students will score 80% or higher in reading, as measured by the common assessment established in our PLC.
- Middle School/Junior High: By the end of the unit on ratios, 85% of my sixth-grade students will score 80% or higher on the assessment for "understanding ratios and use ratio language to describe a ratio relationship between two quantities." For example, "The ratio of wings to beaks in the bird house at the zoo was 2:1, because for every 2 wings there was 1 beak."
- High School: By the end of the 1st quarter, 95% of my 10th-grade students will score at or above proficient in writing organization and conventions as measured by the district-level writing assessments.

Asking the Right Questions to Help Focus Efforts

In prioritizing the curriculum and scheduling, the principal, as instructional leader, must begin by posing a series of questions to ensure that the correct focus and target are being addressed. I am reminded of a late winter night a few years ago when I took my wife to the hospital for lower back pains. The staff asked many questions to narrow the endless possibilities until they felt confident in their primary diagnosis of kidney stones. I wondered why the staff had asked those specific initial questions.

I began to think about the process they used and realized it didn't matter what they initially might have thought, because there were endless possibilities. What mattered was what happened when they involved my wife. They inquired, assessed, combined what they knew with current circumstances, and used the results to target their work and ultimately, fix the problem. A light bulb went off and I determined this is why instructional leaders must come outside of their heads and pose the right questions when prioritizing their work.

I learned that I needed to communicate to others that, although everything is important, not all things are as urgent as others. As you plan, think about your plan as if it required a sense of urgency. School leaders must have a sense of urgency to improve the lives of those that desperately rely on them everyday to provide them with a better tomorrow. In my quest to prioritize my work for greater student achievement, I created a priorities checklist. These priorities assisted me in determining my building's focus and setting school-wide goals and teacher targets.

Priorities Checklist

- Complete a comprehensive needs assessment based on trend data
- Assess the learning environment, discipline and attendance
- Assess the culture of the learning environment

- Assess the effectiveness of technology and learning
- Assess if methods and materials are scientifically based and empirically sound
- Assess the homeostasis of change
- Assess the current majority
- Assess the factors (i.e., data, rhetoric) that drive decisions
- Assess the amount of time and effectiveness of staff collaboration in PLCs
- Assess the quality of teaching and learning time
- Assess how time is used to improve student achievement
- Assess how the curriculum has been prioritized
- Assess accountability from the smallest to largest unit (i.e., students by teacher in the building, grade level in the building, grade level across the district)
- Assess the current support services and available resources
- Assess the building and district focus and its alignment with school processes

"The toughest thing in education is being honest. A key to the success of any plan, and/or any reform, starts with everyone being honest."

—Jake Hudson, Ty's Mentor

In collaborating with colleagues I found that many instructional leaders need support when establishing and prioritizing goals. Begin the tough conversations, and remember to include these pointers:

- Celebrate success first
- Maintain the dignity of the employee during the conversations
- Use data and not thoughts or opinions
- Be consistent
- Tie performance to the conversation of goals and targets
- Offer suggestions for improvement
- Give access to resources
- Give them hope but be clear on consequences
- Tie their performance to school-wide goals and targets to show the importance of individual efforts
- Establish a feedback system or process with timelines and hold to it

Our Initial Leadership Priorities

Finally, leaders must ensure their priorities are based on real-time data and include all stakeholders. They must be communicated and monitored consistently. This opens the door to creating powerful strategies to achieve the desired outcomes and levels of accountability to support continual improvement. The list below contains our initial leadership priorities. This list was narrowed as we moved through the year. I would suggest limiting these and assigning key people to monitor and report out on each area as part of the ongoing data collection process.

1. Determine academic content areas with the greatest discrepancies between student data and intended outcomes.
2. Develop a building-level CIP with input from staff to address areas with greatest discrepancies.
3. Create action strategies and evaluation strategies for each goal.
4. Design structured staff collaboration time and activities that follow the PLC process.
5. Have teachers serve as a responsible mentor for each assigned student.
6. Provide additional quality instructional time for at-risk students, including extended day programming all year.
7. Provide teaching models that support individualized skill development.
8. Select empirically sound teaching and learning methods/materials/supports.
9. Complete a simplistic multiple progression model to elevate effects of methods and materials.
10. Provide long-term diagnostic assessments to determine need and to measure progress/growth over time.
11. Select diagnostic and prescriptive materials and resources that allow teachers to teach for mastery.
12. Use short-cycle common formative assessments to measure objective mastery.
13. Use the PLC collaboration model to determine the building calendar and instructional focus.
14. Create a new majority by starting with open and honest conversations.
15. Build a school-wide accountability model.
16. Prioritize the curriculum based on the question, *"What should students know and be able to do at the end of the day/week/month/quarter/semester/school year?"*
17. Teach test preparation action vocabulary in all content areas.
18. Teach non-fiction writing in all content areas.
19. Provide long-term early intervention to close achievement gaps.
20. Provide test intervention services from the cut line down.
21. Provide a learning prescription, or Individualized Academic Plan, for each student based on current assessment data.
22. Provide sustained staff development on differentiated instruction and classroom management techniques tied to instruction.

Cylinder 3: Scheduling the Right School-Wide Intervention

"The need for intervention focused on motivating older, struggling readers is clear. The National Assessment of Educational Progress has reported that two-thirds of America's eighth- and 12th-grade students are not proficient in reading."

—Steve McClung

Schools often have a difficult time determining how to schedule school-wide interventions so that they effectively maximize student learning. The process of mandating "cookie-cutter" techniques to solve every problem without regard for the individuals being impacted is inappropriate and indicative of a system that may not be completely student-driven. In order to achieve the desired performance outcomes developed in the continual improvement plan, there must be a site-specific and student-specific intervention plan that includes relevant enrichment, maintenance and remediation opportunities for all students.

Processes and procedures need to be created to ensure standards are not just taught, but are mastered. There is a simple saying that we share with teachers nationwide, *"If students aren't learning then you aren't teaching."* The result of teaching is learning! Anything short of that is simply covering the material. There must be a procedure developed to ensure the following:

- students learn and can demonstrate independently mastery of the standard;
- intervention is provided immediately to students not mastering the standard; and
- extension, mastery retention and maintenance are a priority once students have consistently demonstrated they can perform independently.

Another difficult yet important task for principals and staff is determining which interventions best meet the needs of the school and scheduling all of the interventions that must occur during the school day. At Crestwood Elementary, Scott scheduled all of the following school-wide interventions:

- reading intervention,
- developmental math,
- English Language Learners (ELL) class,
- Additional School Instruction (ASI),
- speech and language,
- special education resource time, and
- other special education classes such as occupational therapy and physical therapy.

School-wide interventions are a critical component to student success. School-wide interventions can occur before, during or after school and are based on available resources and supports.

These interventions are designed to accelerate and/or maintain student learning for high-end student achievers, middle of the road students and for students that need additional reinforcements and supports. The scheduled intervention groups are flexible and can change over time. In practice, we reorganized monthly and/or as needed based on specific skills that needed to be mastered. Developing an appropriate school, grade-level and individual intervention plan is essential in providing the necessary support and resources to teachers and students.

"We could learn a lot from crayons; some are sharp, some are pretty, some are dull, some have weird names, some are more popular than others—but they all have to learn to live in the same box."

—Author Unknown

Every school-based teacher has to face the challenges associated with educating all types of students in one classroom every day. Regardless if students are scheduled hetero- or homogeneously, there are rarely any concepts that all students will master the same way or at the same time. This means there will always be a need to provide interventions that provide support to those who simply don't get it. Because we have bright students, unmotivated students, low-performing students, students who seem to just not care, and students who struggle to get along with others, we have to be engaging and timely in our implementation of intervention services. Although many have talked about this type of individualized contact for years, it is seldom seen in the classroom because the concept implies that teachers must develop multiple lesson plans on a regular basis. Our task is to recognize that we have all types of students and we must learn to teach all of them at their own level in the same environment through school-wide and classroom interventions.

The following section provides examples and explanations of the programs used to impact change at Crestwood Elementary. Although the example is that of an elementary school, the programs can be easily adapted for use in any secondary school environment.

Scott's Thoughts: Scheduling Can Be a Nightmare!

After determining what areas we needed to address, it was time to figure out when and how to get it all done. It proved very difficult to create schedules for all of the necessary interventions; however the process had to be completed and implemented with fidelity. Scheduling became even more difficult because many students at Crestwood needed four or more of these pull-out intervention classes based on various data sources.

To address this challenge, I created a new plan for developing our intervention schedule. It was fantastic! Each classroom teacher turned in a schedule with their first, second and third choice for pull-outs. Teacher involvement in selecting what was best for the students created a sense of power and ownership that set the tone for establishing a culture of shared vision by a committed staff. Intervention choices were determined based on the review of school-wide data trends and other classroom assessment information.

I crafted a large schedule on poster-board highlighting each teacher's data-driven intervention preferences along with their desired intervention times. Teachers in each grade level met with me and the designated teachers for reading intervention, developmental math, ELL, and special education to ensure they had selected the best intervention and could articulate the implementation plan they had developed. All six grade levels (K–5) met separately with our intervention staff and every pull-out intervention was able to be scheduled into each of the teachers' top three choices. Frankly, I was shocked and amazed by how well this method worked.

Accelerated Reader

Accelerated Reader (AR) is a program designed to motivate students to read. When students read an AR book, they take a computer-based quiz to test their comprehension of the book. Each student, in consultation with their teacher, sets a goal each quarter as to how many AR books they will read during the quarter. When they reach 100% of their goal they enjoy their next visit to the library where they will select a brand new book for their own personal book collection. For those students who really excel to meet 200% of their goal, they would come to my office to select a book for them to take home and enjoy. It was a pleasure for me to write a note of congratulations in their new books.

Developmental Math

Developmental Math was offered to students in grades two through five who struggled in mathematics. Based on the previous year's MAP (Missouri Assessment Program) math scores and other assessments, students were selected to receive additional learning time each day. Math interventionists worked with students in small groups for 30 minutes per day. The Developmental Math curriculum was separate but interdependent with the classroom curriculum. At Crestwood, we had two teachers who spent half of their day providing Developmental Math instruction.

English Language Learners Program

Crestwood had one of the finest English Language Learners (ELL) programs that I have ever encountered. We had a wonderful full-time ELL teacher and one full-time teaching assistant who worked with many students who arrived at our school not being able to speak any English. The key to hiring an ELL teacher is to hire a teacher with a fabulous background in literacy instruction. That is exactly what we did and it was a key reason why our ELL students achieved at such a high level. Our ELL teacher scheduled all of our ELL students for 30 minutes or more per day in a small-group instructional setting, in which all of the instruction was in English.

The teaching assistant spent most of her day pushing into our classrooms. With nearly 60 ELL students, representing 16 foreign countries, we provided support to each of our grade levels and classrooms. Our teaching assistant was also a certified teacher who received a great deal of professional development and training to work with ELL students. In addition to our ELL assistant pushing into classrooms and students receiving direct instruction from our ELL teacher in a pull-out, small-group setting, we were able to offer full-day kindergarten to all ELL kindergartners free of charge. Full-day kindergarten (tuition based in our district) gave ELL students a great head start on becoming more familiar with the English language, literacy and math skills.

Some of the keys for success with ELL students include:

- Providing early, explicit and intensive instruction in phonological awareness and phonics, in order to build decoding skills. ELLs in primary grades should have an extended literacy block.
- Increasing opportunities for ELLs to develop vocabulary knowledge.
- Using reading instruction to equip ELLs with strategies and knowledge that allow them to comprehend and analyze challenging texts.
- Providing opportunities for ELLs to engage in structured, academic talk.
- Structuring purposeful independent reading.
- Providing early, explicit and intensive instruction and intervention in basic mathematics concepts and skills.
- Focusing on academic language in mathematics. It is a significant source of difficulty for many ELLs who struggle with mathematics.
- Providing academic language support so ELLs can understand and solve word problems that are often used for mathematics assessment and instruction.
- In Lindbergh Schools we were fortunate to have the leadership of Dr. Nancy Rathjen who served as our Assistant Superintendent of Curriculum and Instruction. She was an expert in her knowledge of ELL instruction and had a strong background in literacy instruction. We were able to truly benefit students because of her knowledge of ELL instructional best practices.

At Crestwood, our ELL staff worked and communicated very well with our classroom teachers. When students struggled with specific concepts in the classroom, the ELL staff was notified and they targeted the students' deficiencies. When students began to make progress, they were motivated to work even harder. **"If students are motivated to learn the content in a given subject, their achievement in that subject will most likely be good. If students are not motivated to learn the content, their achievement will likely be limited"** (Marzano, 2003, p. 144).

Additional School Instruction (ASI)

One of our most important school-wide interventions was After-School Instruction and Additional School Instruction. At Crestwood these programs, specifically targeted to third- through fifth-grade students (MAP-tested grade levels), differed from our reading and math interventions. Additional School Instruction is just another name for site-based tutoring. Each classroom in a MAP grade had a 30-minute time slot available for classroom teachers to send students to work with a math or reading tutor to improve skills in specific targeted areas. If only four students did not understand a concept, instead of re-teaching this concept to the entire class, the small group of targeted students would receive instruction from their ASI tutor.

Because our classroom teachers were willing to work in our after-school program, they already understood the needs of our students and could create lessons to give students additional support that they could not receive during the school day. One of our After-School Instructors shared the following strategy:

> Quite often, I will say to the students: "I am going to let you in on a little secret. Tomorrow, I am going to teach you a new concept. Today I am going to give you a head start, but you cannot tell your classmates." Then I preview the next day's lesson with these students. Many times when I begin instruction on a new concept, the higher students in the class will not be able to answer questions about this new concept. They are impressed when some of our lower-performing students are able to answer the question. In fact, sometimes they marvel at the level of their peers' knowledge. This is fun for me, but you should see what it does to boost the self-esteem of some of my struggling students.

This is a great strategy—not only does it give many of our struggling students a head start, but most of these students experience a boost in their self-esteem and confidence when it comes to academics.

Cathy's Commentary: Scheduling Strategies

One challenge many leaders face when looking at incorporating interventions into the regular school day is breaking the traditional school schedule. It is imperative that we realize and get others to embrace the concept that school, the way we have always known it, must change. It is not uncommon to hear teachers, parents and school leaders discuss the stark differences between students today and those of the past; however, we have taken great pride in teaching today's students the same way we did those students from years ago. As leaders focus on moving schools forward, we must be mindful of the training needed to do things differently.

As you begin to schedule your interventions, ask yourself what might a school-wide intervention schedule look like in your building? Determine if you will use computer-based programs as part of your school-wide intervention program. Implementers of computer-based programs should ask if the program is diagnostic and prescriptive, as it is important to document observable and measurable student short- and long-term growth gains. It is important to note that computer-based software may be utilized to assist in delivering sound instruction based on prescriptive data and short- or long-term objective mastery.

Scheduling meaningful interventions requires you to understand the dynamics of the building and honestly evaluate the impact of what you are currently doing. For instance, if you offer a Saturday school and only seven students participate or there is no real remediation of targeted deficits, this intervention program should be dissolved. Shifting to include the most impactful strategies for many might include a school-based structural change. Structural changes come in many forms. If we make better decisions on how we place students in classes, what teachers are placed with what students, where teachers are placed in the building, and how much time students spend focusing on the skills they need, we will notice an increase in student learning. The days of "years of service" dictating what teachers will teach, as if time equals quality or automatically gives a teacher the right to teach the "good classes" are long gone. Data must determine how we schedule students, teachers and meaningful interventions.

It is important to note that structural changes are easily developed and observed; however, quite often, they do not lead to attitudinal changes in staff members. Leaders must involve teachers in the process of change to ensure their understanding and commitment to the changes that must occur. We have found that being transparent and using data to determine the "why" of the work assists teachers in understanding structural changes and intervention strategies. If they understand it, we have a greater chance of them buying into the change effort.

Ty's Take: Extreme Schedule Design in a School to Watch

The staff worked collaboratively with administration in the scheduling process. In creating the master schedule they decided that collaborating early in the school year and using common assessment data to prioritize the schedule, would be key and instrumental for a successful upcoming school year. With this in mind, administration provided the staff scheduling parameters and the scheduling process began.

Our Guiding Design Parameters for the Master Schedule:

- Math taught daily to every student.
- Ability to double block classes on each grade level team if desired.

- Acceleration and enrichment opportunities provided during the regular school day for all students.
- Special Education intervention would be on a consultancy basis.
- The master schedule would have the ability for administration to conduct Seminars/ Town Meetings with students, without disrupting the core academic school day.
- Collaborative team and department planning times would occur daily during the school day.
- No study halls would be assigned as the day had been compressed due to budgetary constraints.

The administrative team modeled practices in weekly staff meetings that they had read about in PLC guidebooks. The premise behind their sharing of information and involving staff from the beginning was simple; to obtain buy-in and earn trust. School leaders are reminded that no matter how many times you state to your staff that they had a clean sheet of paper to work from, there will be some skepticism. School leaders must continually work to earn the teachers trust. I provided the administrative team and staff members with parameters for the schedule based on conversations, big ideas, and questions posed by Rick DuFour, Robert Eaker, Rebecca DuFour and Harvey Silver (personal communication, July 2007).

The "Big Ideas" posed by DuFour, Eaker and DuFour in creating a successful schedule were:

- Teaching Versus Learning: Removing instructional barriers for teachers to improve student achievement; staff members heard instructional barriers spoken, however they internalized structural barriers. As the instructional leader, I determined I could only hold myself accountable, as I had not provided clarity in understanding. What might I have done differently? I could have checked for understanding, similar to what I had asked my teachers to do in their classrooms daily after instructing students. This is a reminder to administrators and instructional leaders to check and inspect what you expect. Do not assume on face value that individuals truly understand your message.
- Collaboration: Schedule and honor time to meet and discuss the diverse needs of staff and students. In my first years of administration I can truly say that many of my staff meetings were filled with conversation. These conversations took us as a staff no closer to improving student achievement, and we might have been better off not meeting at all. "Collaborative" meetings in regard to the schedule were going well. Focused meetings gave staff a common purpose and goal.
- Using Data to Drive Instructional and Structural Decisions: Improving classroom instructional practices and the use of common assessment data were essential in planning and implementing a successful school-wide intervention plan and scheduling instructional interventions. All students in the school were to receive acceleration, enrichment, and maintenance services. Students who met a specific standard, normally above 70% on a pre-assessment, were placed in enrichment interventions, while

those not meeting the standard were placed in a class that focused on specific content. These student groupings were flexible allowing students to move in and out based on assessment data and as instructional needs changed.

The following questions were posed by Harvey Silver:

- How would you design a schedule that motivates staff and students; that was manageable and provided multiple opportunities for staff and students to achieve at high levels?
- How would your school become a professional learning community that supports the improvement process, enabling the greatest gains in student performance?

After hearing the questions posed by Silver, a scheduling committee was formed allowing the administration team to work with others on creating a schedule that would address their ideas and questions. This marked the birth and creation of a rigorous and comprehensive "Extreme Design" schedule for raising student achievement. Collaboratively they determined that there were factors that would enhance the probability of their success. These factors included:

- Collaboration among staff about individual students.
- Support and accountability for all student achievement must begin with the regular classroom teacher.
- At-risk children receiving additional quality teaching time, before, during and after-school if feasible.
- Everyone in the building is responsible for the success of every student in the school.
- Using data and prioritizing what is needed to achieve (focus); sharing ideas about what worked and did not work, and why (collaboration and reflection); and by using measurements/results in planning for the future student success (adaptation and timely response).

Cylinder 4: Getting Results Through a Grade-Level Intervention Plan

"The earlier we intervene, the better off the community is and the individual. The way we break this cycle is education, intervention and collaboration."

—Diane Balkin

Leaders at all levels often overlook the importance of providing grade-level interventions and collaborative planning time during the regular school day. Finding a way to provide this honored time and to integrate data supported interventions will go a long way with teachers and students. These two things, when structured appropriately, are essential because they allow staff to dig deeper into student work products, plan common lessons and assignments for further analysis of student learning and to make adjustments in instruction to meet the individual needs of their students. This may even mean shifting teachers and students based on teachers' strengths. Students benefit tremendously when teachers talk to each other about what they can do to reach a student instead of focusing only on students' shortcomings.

How to Get Results Through a Grade-Level Intervention Plan

A grade-level intervention plan is grade-level specific, and based on the skill which students lack. Student data is used in determining which skills were mastered and which skills need review and/or remediation. To be most effective, grade-level intervention plans must focus on the student's ability to demonstrate proficiency based on the benchmarks or performance standards they are expected to master during the current term. Unlike the school-wide intervention plan, which is designed to address school-wide deficits or areas in need of change, the grade-level plan narrows the focus of each teacher based on the performance indicators connected to the subject and grade taught. School-based leaders should take precautions to avoid common pitfalls such as developing grade-level interventions based on school-wide data. We must always ensure interventions prepare students for their personal assessment as well as for meeting school or district targets—one without the other is a recipe for disaster.

Teachers must become experts on what students must know and be able to do by the time they complete the school year. They must look at targets based on the students they teach and be willing to adjust immediately in order to handle deficits in both teaching and learning. The targeted grade-level plan must include systems for providing immediate feedback and interventions based on grade-specific state standards, benchmarks, and performance indicators. Leaders must provide teachers and students with the necessary support and resources to achieve the desired outcomes developed in the overall continual improvement plan. When leaders and teachers design and schedule a grade-level intervention period, it must be designed to provide enrichment, maintenance and remediation opportunities for all students. Because these groups are fluid and based solely on each student's ability to demonstrate independent proficiency, managing them must be done carefully and with sincere commitment from teachers, students and other school leaders.

Administrators are instrumental in the overall success of any plan put forth in the building. It is critical that administrators are actively monitoring, providing feedback to teachers and students, modeling strategies, and ensuring the teams are implementing grade-level and school-wide strategies with fidelity.

Scott's Thoughts: Success with Interventions at Crestwood

"The most obvious impediment to a results orientation is the failure at the beginning of the year to put the data in front of the teachers, have them look at it and then generate a manageable number of measurable goals based on the previous year's scores. That should be job one for administrators."

—Michael Schmoker, 2002

Michael Schmoker characterizes one of the keys to continual school improvement. As mentioned previously, to continue to improve, schools must focus on their achievement data, find their strengths and weaknesses, and create plans to improve upon their weaknesses. This should take place during the summer or as early in the school year as possible.

As the principal, I met with each grade level in grades 3–5 early in September, in order to review state testing results from the previous year. If teachers are to have the necessary impact on subgroup students, they must review data early to ensure that they are most effective, especially with their at-risk students. *Early intervention is extremely important!*

The better we do at the elementary level with our most at-risk students, the better prepared these students will be when they reach middle and high school. **"At age 17, the typical black or Hispanic student is scoring well less on the nation's most reliable tests than at least 80% of his or her white classmates. In five of the seven subjects tested by the National Assessment of Educational Progress (NAEP), a majority of black students perform in the lowest category—below basic. The result: By 12th grade, African-Americans are typically four years behind white and Asian students. These students are finishing high school with a junior high education"** (Thernstrom & Thernstrom, 2003, p. 2).

One of the greatest challenges schools face is reducing the achievement gap. **"Most Americans assume that the low achievement of poor and minority children is bound up in the children themselves or their families. 'The children don't try.' 'They have no place to study.' 'Their parents don't care.' 'Their culture doesn't value education.' These and**

other excuses are regularly offered up to explain the achievement gap that separates poor and minority students from other young Americans" (Williams, 2003, p. 3).

Your State Department of Education most likely provides Item Benchmark Descriptors (IBD) data. The IBD data reveal which skills and concepts our students know well and which areas are weak. Each grade level examines its weaknesses and creates improvement plans to help students comprehend these difficult areas. Every month, teachers from each grade level would meet with me to critically examine our progress with student achievement. During these meetings, it was important for me to have knowledge about each of our individual students.

Monthly Meetings Lead to Success

"Effective schools do not follow the 'sink or swim' approach. Nor do they wade in to rescue students only when they have proven they can't swim. Schools that are committed to success for all students systematically identify struggling students. They identify problems as early as possible—well before students have a chance to fail" (Blankstein, 2004, p. 112).

Sample Intervention Outline:

September

- How did last year's students perform on state testing?
- How close were our predictions compared to testing results?
- Why did specific students do better or worse than expected?
- Based on the IBD data, what are our strengths and weaknesses?
- How are our subgroups performing?
- Which students need individual attention regarding instruction, work ethic, behavior, etc . . . ?

October/November/December

- Review previous months' eValuate Assessment (product of Catapult Learning) results and IBD data.
- How do students' eValuate reading scores compare with their math scores?
- Determine high/low performing students as well as those on the bubble.
- Are students progressing like they should?
- Which students need to participate in after school instruction?
- Who do teachers want me to talk to about behavior, attendance, effort?

January

The key this month is for teachers to make a prediction for each student. Each teacher needs to assess each student's chances for scoring proficiency on state testing, and evaluate whether students will meet their goal. "Yes" means that a particular student will score proficient, "maybe" means the child has a chance, and "no" means the student is not yet capable of scoring proficient. Many of these students may not be grade proficient as a third-grader, but with continued use of strategies, interventions, and great teaching, the student will have a better chance in subsequent grades.

If a student receives all "maybes" and "noes" talk about whether he or she should start attending after school instruction. Some parents feel offended when we encourage their child to attend and think we are saying their child is a weak student. We remind parents that this additional instruction is designed to assist students achieve at a higher level.

- Review previous semesters eValuate Assessment results and IBD data.
- How do students' eValuate reading scores compare with their math scores?
- Determine high/low performing students as well as those on the bubble.
- Are students progressing like they should?
- Which students need to participate in after school instruction?
- Who do the teachers want me to talk to about behavior, attendance, effort?

February

- With state testing around the corner, review IBD data to make sure teachers have covered all of their weak areas.
- Review previous month's eValuate Assessment results, IBD data and cumulative results.
- How do students' eValuate reading scores compare with their math scores?
- Determine high/low performing students as well as those on the bubble.
- Are students progressing like they should?
- Which students need to participate in after school instruction?
- Who do teachers want me to talk to about behavior, attendance, effort?
- Support teachers in assisting students to attain 80% achievement on eValuate tests three times, which practically guarantees state testing success.
- Make preliminary plans for state testing schedule.

March

- Look at the cumulative eValuate results.
- Review IBD data to make sure teachers have covered all of their weak areas. MAP testing is only a few weeks away.

- Analyze collective data for each student and share predictions. (I recommend a color coded system with predictions by grade level.)
- Who do the teachers want me to talk to about behavior, attendance, effort?
- Finalize the schedule for state testing?

Preparing for the State Test

I met with each grade level in February to create their state testing schedule. During this meeting, we discussed each student and examined strategies to support their best performance.

- In third and fourth grade, there are six different tests administered in communication arts and math. Which test do we want to take first?
- In fifth grade there are nine different test sections administered in communication arts, math and science. How can we schedule creatively to reduce burnout? Can we accelerate the test-taking?
- Do we have students who would do better in the afternoon, or would they have more success in the morning?
- Which students would do better if tested in a small-group setting?
- How do we adapt our art, music, and P.E. schedule to benefit testing?
- Is a proctor needed during testing? Would students benefit from a proctor being present?
- Would having snacks available during testing support student achievement? There are multiple theories relating to the presence of different foods being offered during testing, including fruits and mints.

A Culture of Collaboration

Each grade-level teacher spent quality time each month meeting in a PLC. Each grade level created SMART goals at the beginning of the year, which are monitored for progress throughout the year. Rick DuFour, for whom "vision" is a mantra, believes that the fastest route to vision is data analysis, and goal setting, because these processes define and make the vision concrete (Schmoker, 2001). During PLC time, teachers strategize with regard to improving student achievement, discuss interventions to help struggling students and collaborate on best practices and lesson plans. Quite often, as I would walk down the hallway at 5 p.m., a few hours after dismissal, I would find grade levels still meeting and working as teams to plan common assessments and lesson plans. Schools and teams that get results work collaboratively and are committed to working together to move every student. *The key to gaining consistency is developing and maintaining a common language of instruction.*

I have visited many schools where collaboration is not a part of the school culture. The key to collaboration is creating an environment that is non-competitive and non-threatening. Fullan and Stiegelbauer discovered that teachers seem to learn best in an environment where they learn from one another. In a truly collaborative, non-competitive setting, teachers are much more willing to share their ideas with others. This practice leads to improved student learning and increases achievement. The finest teachers are those who seek out the best methods of instruction in their classrooms and then share those ideas with their colleagues. Everyone in the organization is expected to be constantly in a teaching and learning mode. True learning takes place only when the leader/teacher invests the time and emotional energy to engage those around him or her in a dialogue that produces mutual understanding (Tichy and Cohen, 1997).

Implementing a Grade-Level Intervention Plan

A well-developed strategic grade-level intervention plan that allows collaboration is the glue that holds the many pieces together. The focus is to ensure every student gains additional quality teaching on an as needed basis. You should not be interested in providing more of the same, or doing things the way they have always been done, because it is obvious that these things did not work. This may be a difficult reality, but with using data, you will garner support and eventually commitment.

A grade-level intervention plan must be:

- scientifically based;
- empirically sound;
- based on the utilization of proven methods and materials;
- observable and measurable; and
- the road to short- and long-term mastery of key concepts.

At Crestwood, we set out to ensure that teachers were scaffolding to have students performing at the level of mastery, and not reducing the level of rigor, which gave both the teacher and the student a false sense of success. Teachers had to teach every student at grade-level or above, providing the support and background information needed to make this possible.

Ty's Take: Building Bridges

Why is teaching on grade-level important? According to my colleague, Dr. Michael White (personal communication, 2010) teaching on grade-level is important for several reasons:

- Students perform no higher than the assignment given.
- State tests assess grade-level content.
- Students cannot learn what they're not taught.
- Students learn more when taught at a higher level than at a lower level.

Will These Kids Ever Get There?

We have to train ourselves to set a standard and build a bridge, through targeted instruction, to get students over to the other side. We then have to care enough about the students to hold them accountable for your higher standards until they make those high standards their own. *Students must work independently and consistently at the level of expected performance.*

Interventions should be scientifically based and provide empirically sound methods and materials. Re-teaching during grade-level intervention periods does not look like teaching in the regular education classroom. Albert Einstein believed the definition of insanity is doing the same thing over and over again and expecting a different result. A teacher re-teaching a class lesson at a slower pace and/or at a higher volume level as the intervention cannot expect students to learn and understand the material better. There is no benefit to giving a student 100 multiplication facts in an effort to ensure he or she understands the concept. Although practice and assessment are very important, a quality intervention is much more than that.

We found that our students needed quality teaching time. This is time when students are actively involved in learning developmentally appropriate materials. If quality-teaching time is used correctly, it will accelerate student learning. Providing additional quality-teaching time during and outside of the school day are two ways to accelerate learning. Quality teaching yields results. Marzano's research found that two teachers working with the same socioeconomic population can achieve vastly different results on the same test. In one class, only 27% of the students will pass the test while in another, 72% will pass (2001).

A grade-level intervention plan includes the following:

- a data review;
- the standards that will be taught;
- assessments based on the performance objectives to be mastered according to state standards;
- student needs;
- a beginning and ending date for assessments;
- the materials, resources and supports that will be needed;
- who will provide instruction and to what students (enrichment, maintenance and remediation); and
- when the intervention instruction will take place (before, during and/or after school).

Cylinder 5: Creating and Using Intervention Notebooks

"What happened to the children? Do you mean you spent a billion dollars and you don't know whether they can read or not?"
—Senator Robert F. Kennedy

School data and other documentation is often not organized in a meaningful or user-friendly way. In order to implement appropriate interventions and to maintain the necessary documentation for accountability, teachers and administrators need to be able to have a consistent, centralized system for collecting, monitoring, managing and using real-time data to inform instructional practice and determine appropriate interventions. Utilizing a school-wide system allows for consistent collection and monitoring, and allows staff to speak the same language.

In the age of increased accountability the idea of maintaining documentation of your efforts to move students forward is a must. An intervention notebook, also referred to as a data notebook, or evidence folder, equips administration, staff and students with a systemic method for documenting teacher efforts and monitoring individual student growth.

The intervention notebook makes daily, weekly, monthly and quarterly monitoring easier and more comprehensive. Intervention notebooks are essential to documenting and monitoring if the prescribed plan is assisting administration, teachers and students in reaching their desired goals. A SMART plan is included to frame individual enrichment and remediation efforts based on the following intervention components:

- test intervention
- skills intervention
- enrichment intervention
- short-term assessments
- prioritized standards and benchmarks
- disaggregated student data
- progress-monitoring documents
- student specific data such as IEP, 504, or Conditions of Learning

Teachers maintain this information on each of their students and use it during conferences, goal setting, and in their PLCs. This allows them to track trend data in one place, monitor what is working and what is not working, and make changes immediately based on real-time data. Additionally, these notebooks provide teachers with documentation of their intervention efforts.

Scott's Thoughts: The Benefit of an Intervention Notebook

Intervention notebooks are a terrific concept and continued to evolve during my time at Crestwood. Crestwood's Intervention Notebook started out as an Intervention Document that looked like this:

Name	IEP	Free/Red	AA	ELL	NEW	SEPT.	NOV.	JAN.	MAR.
Stud. 1	X	X				60	45	60	75
Stud. 2		X	X	X		40	50	80	75
Stud. 3	X	X			X	50	40	70	40
Stud. 4			X	X	X	60	60	50	80
Stud. 5				X	X	80	80	90	80
Stud. 6	X		X			50	50	60	75

Figure 10: Sample Intervention Document

This chart was designed to document interventions offered to students, their subgroup status, and their monthly testing scores. At monthly grade-level meetings, discussions occurred regarding at-risk students and their testing scores. Like Schmoker, we found that few things are more motivating than to receive short-term feedback on how we are progressing toward our goals (2001). Using this format, we were able to track each of our subgroups and discuss how we could help students improve their achievement level. Before No Child Left Behind (NCLB), schools rarely disaggregated their scores or discussed and evaluated how their "subgroup" students were performing. If you have always worked in schools with very little poverty, it is possible that you have not experienced firsthand how difficult it is for some students from poverty to learn. A few years ago, each of the Lindbergh elementary school principals were given a packet of information about our students who attended preschool at the Lindbergh Early Childhood Center. This is a fee-based preschool, and many Crestwood families cannot afford the tuition. I was handed a packet with information on six students, while another principal from my district received a packet with information on more than 30 students. Most of our incoming kindergarten students do not know how to read, let alone the letters of the alphabet. Our kindergarten teachers have a difficult job of catching students up to their peers in other schools who have had the advantage of attending preschool.

As educators, we know there have been numerous studies highlighting the key effects of early childhood education and how early interventions and instruction can prepare students for the start of school. Using information such as that provided by the preschool in our intervention planning and including it in our notebook allowed us to use data to identify our at-risk population and helped us focus on individual students as well as the grade level as a whole. One of the great things about NCLB is that we were forced to disaggregate our data and focus on our subgroup student achievement using information instead of stereotypes and assumptions. In 2001, U.S. Secretary of Education Rod Paige stated, **"If you don't assess where you are, what the students have learned or not learned, you are teaching in the dark. That's analogous to driving at night without headlights"** (Thernstrom & Thernstrom, 2003, p. 3).

Understanding the dynamics of various subgroups helps to ensure the inclusion of appropriate interventions. A number of years ago, I was talking with a principal from a neighboring district, and she told that her school had the highest math MAP scores in the district. I congratulated her on the accomplishment and then asked her what percentage of free/reduced students she had in her school. She responded, *"What does that have to do with anything?"* Obviously, she did not understand that poverty is a key factor in predicting student achievement. **"What works in a wealthy suburb may not work in an urban center or a region of rural poverty"** (Blankstein, 2010, p. 55). This is why it is so important to find interventions that work for our students and not just use what someone else had found to be successful in other environments.

Notebooks Support Response to Intervention or Similar Processes

As a part of the Response to Intervention (RtI) process, we created more elaborate intervention folders. In the past, I would sit in grade-level meetings and a teacher would ask if a specific student had ever been recommended for academic screenings or language evaluations. A common response was "I am not sure," or "I will have to ask his teacher from last year." Once we created our Intervention Folders, all of that information was readily available, including report cards, testing results and teacher notes. When our RtI team would meet to discuss a particular student, the intervention folder was accessible and helped us understand the student's educational background. Although programs like RtI are invaluable in the long run, the implementation of those programs is difficult on any staff. As we know, teachers have very difficult jobs, and each time another program is added to their plate, their level of stress increases. Having all of their data decision-making information at their fingertips will help keep teachers organized.

We also utilized grade-level eValuate records in our intervention notebooks. The eValuate data, which included monthly data records for all second through fifth graders, was extremely helpful when discussing a student's achievement level. Quite often in RtI meetings, we shared key eValuate data with the RtI team. If the data showed the student was making progress, it may have helped the team decide whether or not to add additional interventions or proceed with educational testing. If the data showed that the student was not making satisfactory progress, we may have added instructional interventions for the student or pushed the testing timetable forward. It was always important that we kept the focus on our main goal: to teach students the skills that were necessary to move on to middle school, high school, college and a successful career. If we were able to help students achieve on our state achievement test along the way, then that was an added bonus. **"Students who learn only the facts may do well on Jeopardy,**

but the ability to access information and use it practically and creatively is a worthier goal because it is useful throughout life" (Gregory & Chapman, 2002, p. 126).

With expectations rising every year and increased challenges to meet state and national standards, studying student data is essential. Having your data and information in a readily available, user-friendly format is more important than ever.

"In business, I could prove how good I was by the profit that I generated month to month, which improved the bottom line of the corporation. My results were clear and simple and justified my existence in that company. Education, I quickly learned, had no way of giving me that kind of feedback. No elementary teachers with whom I worked or talked really knew how effective they were except for maybe through the limited indicators provided by standardized test scores" (Pollock, 2007, p. 56). Whatever your method of tracking student data and information, whether it be intervention folders, at-risk tables or student achievement data, the key is having current data that is easily accessible and accurate.

Cathy's Commentary: Intervention Notebooks at the Secondary Level

The following is a sample table of contents from a secondary data and intervention notebook used in a Florida high school. This notebook incorporates many of the components listed throughout this book and describes what data is used to make instructional decisions within PLCs. As with other items that we have shared, this could easily be adapted to meet the specific needs of your school.

Data and Intervention Notebook Table of Contents

1. **Prioritized Standards and Benchmarks (based on item specification and current assessment data)**
   - Grade-level expectations/Item Specifications
   - Performance standards (what they must know and be able to do)
   - Standards mastery chart (evidence of 80% mastery per class and remediation of those needing recovery through RtI/DI process)

2. **Current State Assessment Results (Identify/disaggregated by class)**
   - Lowest performing students
   - Bubble (students within 10 points above or below the level of proficiency)
   - Retained (students who have been retained must make a minimum level of growth)
   - Subgroups (divided and listed)
   - Teacher personal assessment results from previous year and Individual Professional Development Plan

- School goals, grade-level goal and personal goal

3. **Other Assessments**
    - Benchmark Assessment Results (by class)
    - Common Assessments/Assignments (samples and results by class/formative and summative)
    - Common Assessment Departmental Comparison (how you match up against your dept.)
    - Scrimmage/In-house Assessment Results

4. **Evidence of Ongoing Use of Reading Enhancement Activities/Strategies, Vocabulary Acquisition Strategies, Writing Across Curriculum (work samples)**

5. **Teacher Resource Section**
    A. Unit Plan—Created collaboratively within the subject area PLC and reviewed by designated administrator, it must follow the appropriate format and include:
        - Common Assessments
        - Unit Project
        - Formative, Interim and Summative Assessments—aligned with standard/benchmark
    B. Daily Lesson Plans with evidence of reflection, specific input and modifications (Figure 11)
        - Differentiated instruction and RtI Interventions listed, use common format (Figure 12)
        - Power standards
        - Lesson objectives, scripted higher order questions, assessment methods, etc.
        - Teacher and student strategies used (must show in student work sample not just in lesson plans)
        - Assessment, reading, writing and instructional strategies
    C. In-Class and External Safety Nets and Recovery Plan (tutoring sign-in sheets, grade recovery plan and usage, for data targeted students—be sure to include your PMPs)
    D. Interventions
        - RtI/DI Interventions (must be shown in student work and lesson plans)
            - Conference Logs (parents and students)
            - Specific interventions for targeted subgroups
            - IEP information by student and modifications, accommodations (must be in plan)
    E. Professional Development information and evidence of usage

Date:	December 3, 2013		Course: Student Research	
Standard(s)	1. Analyze the effect of author's craft on the meaning of a literary text and create a response to literary texts through a variety of methods. 2. Compare and contrast ideas within and across literary texts to make inferences. 3. Analyze the impact of point of view on literary texts.			
Essential Questions	1. How do authors demonstrate universal themes in short stories, myths, and folktales? 2. How do the elements in a short story interact?			
Enduring Knowledge	1. Short stories, myths and folktales are narratives that exhibit specific elements. 2. Authors use literary devices to enhance the story. 3. Short stories myths and folktales exhibit universal themes. 4. The interaction among the elements in a short story, myth and folktale enhances meaning.		**New Vocabulary Terms** 1. Inclination 4. Taciturn 2. Toppled 5. Winced 3. Asylum 6. Exasperation	
Materials Needed	1. Internet-video and model lesson 4. White board 2. Timer 5. Visual Thesaurus 3. Group worksheet 6. Face-Myth-Pandora's Box		7. PowerPoint on Myths and Legends	
Background Knowledge Needed	1. Definition of Myth and Legend 2. Literary Term 3. Using context clues to assign meaning	4. Pandora's Box		

Time	Activity	Teacher notes
Instructional Focus	Literary Analysis	Students may need to review certain literary terms to understand the current concept.
Mini-Lesson	Review the definition of Myth and Legends Discuss the tone used by authors and how point of view impact the story Listen to a song to discuss and identify the elements of a fable or legend Read Pandora's Box.	

Work-Period	**Teacher Activity**	Extensions/Re-teach/ Enrichment: During the work period circulate to support students in groups. Extend/Enrichment: Create a Fable or Legend as a group.
	I do: Read the Myth/Legends "Pandora's Box" and "The Face" to the students and introduce the use of context clues to define new terms in context.	
	We do: Complete a 2nd read of "The Face" allowing students to read portions and discuss preselected words. Discuss defining terms in context and explain your/their thought process.	Re-teach: Discuss the elements and provide additional examples in small groups.
	Student Activity	Differentiation: During small group support, extend.
	We do: Complete a 2nd read of "The Face" and identify the elements that make it a fable or myth. Identify new terms and discuss what makes it a myth or legend.	
		Blooms/Webbs Reference: Application.
	Student Activity	Evaluation/Assessment: Exit ticket: Review a short legend and independently identify what makes it a legend or myth.
	You Do: Students, in groups, go to http://www.americanfolklore.net and choose the myth and legends tab. Choose a story, read, and complete the Legend Study worksheet.	
		Reflections:
Closing/ Wrap-up	Review myths and legends and the tone used in such stories. Complete the exit ticket to assess mastery of today's content.	Homework: Write a myth or legend of your own to teach a moral lesson.

Content-Specific Techniques
___ Vocabulary Strategy: A-Z word sheet; word mapping
___ Reading/Reading Strategy (KWL)
___ Writing Daily/Lab Reports/Word Problems
___ Free Response Writing
_X_ Modeling
___ Other

ESE Accomodations
_X_ Instructional Methods and materials: implements changes to teaching methods
___ Assignments and assessments: changes the way students practice and demonstrate learning in assignments like projects, worksheets, homework and class tests
___ Time demands & scheduling: assists students who need to work at a different pace
___ Learning Environment: maintains a barrier-free classroom
___ Use of special communications system: encourages students

Learning Strategies (Including ESOL)
___ Cornell Notes/ Two Column Notes
___ Skilled Questioning, Socratic Seminars, Quick-write/ Discussion
___ SQ5R, KWL, Think Ahead
_X_ Modified Curriculum: Personalize Lesson
___ Cooperative/Collaborative Learning: peer-tutoring small group work
_X_ Essential vocabulary: identify and teach essential vocabulary
___ Visual Advance Organizers: use visual aids
___ Language Experience Approach
___ Whole language: simplify grammatical structure and paraphrase/summarize sections and highlight or underline key words
_X_ Word Pronunciation & Meaning: Model Key

Figure 11: Sample Lesson Plan
Additional Sample Lesson Plans can be found at www.beyondtheoryedu.com.

In addition to the lesson plan, the RtI/DI section is included in the Intervention Notebook. This indicates what students will do or be given to do differently based on assessment data, benchmarks, exit tickets, etc. These groups are fluid and kids move as they meet mastery performance levels.

Data Utilized to Identify Students for Differentiated Instruction Choose an item. **Marzano's 9 High-Yield Strategies** (circle all that apply)	Differentiated Instruction Small Group – Intensive Assignment(s): Student(s):	Differentiated Instruction Small Group – Proficiency Assignment(s): Student(s):	Differentiated Instruction Small Group – Enrichment Assignment(s): Student(s):
• Identifying Similarities & Differences • Summarizing & Notetaking • Reinforcing Effort/Providing Recognition • Homework & Practice • Nonlinguistic Representations • Cooperative Learning • Setting Objectives & Providing Feedback • Generating & Testing Hypotheses • Cues, Questions & Advance Organizers	1. 2. 3. 4. 5. 6. 7. 8. 9. 10.	1. 2. 3. 4. 5. 6. 7. 8. 9. 10.	1. 2. 3. 4. 5. 6. 7. 8. 9. 10.

Figure 12: RtI/DI Interventions Form

Ty's Take: Listening to Staff Concerns

We have found that when intervention notebooks are utilized by staff, students achieve at higher rates. When we began the intervention notebooks at my school, the staff had many questions related to the purpose and process we were to follow. Many viewed it as "one more thing," because we did not do a good job explaining the benefits before the roll-out. The administration's practice of wavering and not being clear about the expectations relative to how and when the intervention notebooks would be utilized led to some of the frustration and confusion. Listening to the concerns presented by staff and responding in an effort to avoid a mutiny, led to the development of an intervention notebook checklist. Our checklist (Figure 13) outlined what needed to be included and gave examples of what was expected of them to lessen the staff's anxiety. After a short time, teachers found the intervention notebooks have the power to improve teaching and learning. They provide a centralized system for collecting, monitoring, managing and using real-time data to inform instructional decisions and determine appropriate intervention strategies. The notebooks also provided teachers with a portfolio to document their efforts and provide evidence during the evaluation process.

Intervention Notebook Checklist

Teacher: Date:

Form code: Y = yes N = no C = comment required NC = not included E = example required

1. Is the grade-level intervention plan included?

2. Is writing in the content area being implemented?

3. Is the action test vocabulary being taught?

4. Is there an individual objective for each student?

5. Is the beginning date for the objective listed?

6. Are the materials used to teach the objective listed?

7. Is the short-term assessment for each objective listed?

8. Is the ending date for the objective listed?

9. Has the grade-level intervention plan been implemented daily?

10. Principal's comments:

11. Teacher's comments:

Figure 13: Intervention Notebook Checklist

Cylinder 6: Creating a New Majority

"Your attitude speaks so loudly, I can't hear what you are saying."

—Peter Drucker

School culture often reflects an "us versus them" attitude instead of an environment built on mutual support and collaboration. When school staff are not in support of the school goals and mission, it is difficult to create a culture of success, or to routinely see a collaborative environment where the staff is working together to overcome school-wide challenges.

"Three men work in a quarry. When asked what they do for a living, this is how they responded: The first one said, he was a stone-chipper; the second said he cuts marble blocks; but, the third one said, 'I build cathedrals.'"

—Author Unknown

Are the teachers in your school stone-chippers, or are they building cathedrals? Creating a new majority is all about creating a culture of success by building collaborative, collegial, committed relationships that work together to overcome all challenges as a team. By working collaboratively with teachers, school leaders bring down the wall that creates the "us against them" mentality. Operating in this manner helps leaders effectively understand the building needs so they can provide the support necessary to raise student achievement. This process builds pride and wins teachers over one at a time, resulting in overall building success and continual commitment to school improvement. Successful leaders understand the Albert Einstein adage—"not everything that counts can be counted, and not everything that can be counted counts."

Creating a new majority is all about winning over your staff and turning your naysayers into supporters of the school's mission. If this is done correctly there is no limit to what your staff and your students can achieve.

How Creating a New Majority with Teachers and Students Works

A positive school culture leads to commitment and that is what changes things for the better. **"The relationship among adults is an area for potential improvement in a great many schools. While it is relatively easy to install the technical aspects of a professional learning community—systems to collect data, time for teams to meet, etc.—the tough part is subtler, less scripted, and more human"** (Blankstein, 2004, p. 59).

As a leader you must find ways to move people from compliance to commitment. Have you ever walked into a school and known right away that you had entered into a special place? A place where children are eager to learn and teachers love to teach . . . a school where students know their teachers care about them . . . a place where every child belongs to every teacher? *When you enter this building you know great things are inevitable.*

Students must know they are loved and respected and that they have a chance to succeed. The relationships we form with our students are more important than any new best practice we implement, and building positive working relationships among teachers is just as important.

"The relationship among the adults in the schoolhouse has more impact on the quality and the character of the schoolhouse—and on the accomplishments of youngsters—than any other factor" (Barth, 2001, p. 105).

School leaders can help foster high-quality relationships among the adults when they:

- Meet with teachers by grade level, subject area and team.
- Work with teachers individually and show how they impact school improvement.
- Provide support by sharing instructional techniques and materials.
- Help teachers experience success and celebrate small victories.
- Gain teacher commitment to the school's goals and mission.

Schools that make culture a priority have the fuel to power the engine of school improvement. School culture is the key to any improvement effort. There is an old saying, "Children may forget what you teach them, but they will never forget how you treat them." One of the activities I use during workshops with educators is to ask them to recall a great moment from their elementary school years. Most often, the comments are not about getting an "A" on a math test or mastering multiplication facts in third grade. They share a story of a kind act or special day with a teacher. This is because teachers impact students through the tone they set and their ability to make students know they genuinely care about them as people first and then about their achievement. Think back to that teacher who was strict, firm, motherly (or fatherly), and a little demanding . . . he or she was the one whose homework you had to get done, whose class you couldn't skip or show up late to, and whose substitute had minimal problems. *Students can tell if you genuinely care about them, as people and if you are there to make a difference in their lives.*

As teachers and leaders we must be careful with the words we use and the seeds we plant in the minds of our students. Likewise as leaders, we have to remember that teachers and other school-based employees take our words and use them for positive or negative energy. These types of interactions happen every day and help to shape and define classroom and school-wide culture.

If your school starts a new reading program, chances are it will not be successful if teachers are negative about its implementation. Similarly, if teachers are required to put forth extra effort needed to prepare students for state testing, a negative and revolting school culture will interfere and in some cases sabotage even the best initiative. The best way to gain teacher support, commitment, involvement and acceptance of the difficult task of improving student achievement is to seek their input and honor their ideas. Administrators must understand that they do not have all of the answers and that people doing the work may be better able to determine what works and what doesn't. This is critical in gaining buy-in and gives a great boost to climate and culture of the school.

It's been said that "one seldom damns that which he authors," so getting people involved in creating the initiative buys commitment through mere process. As leaders we must understand that getting teachers involved does not lessen your power or authority as a leader but empowers those around you to help you build a strong, impermeable team. Leaders should share different best practices with staff and seek their input as to which ones will best benefit the students in their classrooms. Todd Whitaker's research found that a strong argument could be made that no one is more important in achieving the learning mission of a school than the teacher. At the same time, a school's culture is maintained through the actions of virtually every adult in every role in the school. As a result, the quality of life in a school community is enhanced when all the members of that community understand and accept their roles and responsibilities (2003).

Get Out of the Office

Many principals spend way too much time in their office and not nearly enough time in classrooms. **"Spend more time in schools (if you work in the district) or classrooms (if you are the principal), not just to check up on people, as in the overused management walkthrough, but as a way to develop genuine interest in, curiosity about, and knowledge of what teachers and students are doing. Know your people first. Check the data and spreadsheets second. Not the other way around"** (Blankstein, 2010, p. 235).

With many of the demands now placed on principals this is becoming more and more difficult to do. However, being highly engaged throughout the building has to be a priority. A wonderful goal is to be in every classroom at least twice a day and to greet each staff member and student on a daily basis. This may or may not be possible based on school size and the number of faculty and students you serve. In a small school you may be able to make this your goal but in larger schools you may need to set a rotation schedule to ensure you are in every classroom once a day or once a week. School leaders don't need to feel as if they need to leave a note or documentation with every classroom visit but periodic feedback is valued by the staff.

There is no denying that the more time spent in classrooms getting to know students, the less time students will need to spend in the offices of the administrators. While most principals discourage their teachers from sending students to the office, encourage teachers to send students to see the principal. Teachers really appreciate a supportive principal; their job is too difficult to do without support from leadership, so teachers and principals must work together to build a collaborative, sustainable school environment.

Support Your Teachers

Quite often when we speak to groups of teachers, many of them comment that one of the most difficult parts of their job is that they do not feel supported by their administration. As a school leader seeking to create a new majority, you can never ignore a teacher's request for help. When a teacher sends a student to the office, for instance, administrators must do all that they can to support the teacher whenever possible. If principals send the unwritten message to teachers that they need to handle major disciplinary situations and classroom interruptions on their own, school culture will suffer. Teachers must feel as though their leaders will do whatever they can to help them when they are in need and feel safe asking for support from their peers and their leaders.

When school leaders support teachers, morale will increase. If teachers send students to the office for a serious offense and you do not support them, they will soon lose faith in you as a leader. In addition, if parents are allowed to verbally abuse your teachers on the phone or in person, teacher morale will sink to new depths. If a teacher is talking on the phone and a parent treats them with disrespect, the teacher must be allowed to say that he/she will end the conversation unless the parent speaks in a respectful manner. If the parent continues to be disrespectful, the teacher must understand that he/she is expected to tell the parent to call and set up an appointment with an administrator. Disrespectful parents are not to be tolerated. If a difficult parent wants to meet with a teacher, an administrator should be present at the meeting.

Building Your Team

The hiring process may be a place where teacher teams or other staff need to be involved. We have seen great success in allowing staff to screen applicants and conduct interviews along with administration. Teachers know what they need and can spot things that will cause them problems in the trenches. Using a set of guiding questions and allowing teachers to explain the dynamics of the school, the students, and the team helps to ensure we have the best candidate in front of our students. If you are looking to create a "positive majority" it is vital to always make the right hire.

One of the most important job requirements principals have is hiring new staff. Each new staff member has the potential to add to the positive morale in your building; however, a "bad hire" can further damage your school's culture. **The quickest way to improve your school is to hire great teachers at every opportunity. Just as the only way to improve your average**

grade is to turn in a better-than-average assignment each time, the most significant way to rapidly improve a school is to add teachers who are better than the ones who leave. Great principals know this and work diligently to hire the best possible teachers" (Whitaker, 2003, p. 43).

David Cottrell, in his book entitled *Monday Morning Leadership* (2004), calls this hiring tough. He found that administrators entering new schools inherited the good, the bad, and the ugly. The staff and the culture are already in place, and more often than not, they dig their heels in deep to ensure the new leader doesn't change the "good things" they have going. This makes it all the more important that when there is an opportunity to hire people, it has to be a thoughtful process, where new people are brought in who can positively impact the environment.

If you hire the wrong teacher, you will know it soon. Staff members will come to you quietly and share concerns about their new colleague, and parents will start calling with questions about their child's new teacher. Soon, those questions will become complaints, and before long, you are spending time every day performing damage control. The wrong teacher will kill your momentum and destroy your team.

If you hire the right teacher, it will not be long before your staff members tell you how much they like their new co-worker. Support staff will comment about how well the new teacher fits in and treats everyone with respect. Parents will start calling to tell you how much they like their child's new teacher. Your new hire will get involved, look for ways to support the overall vision and mission of the building, and quickly become committed to the students and their success in school.

Hiring the right teacher is not always easy. During the interview process we must avoid being wowed by past results alone and seek to determine if the candidate will be good for your school and will add to your environment. A good teacher gets results in a particular environment. A great teacher gets results anywhere.

The Right Team

"It's not just about assembling the right team—that's nothing new. The main point is to first get the right people on the bus (and the wrong people off the bus) before you figure out where to drive it" (Collins, 2001, p. 41).

Not only is it important to find staff who will add excellent instruction and positive attitudes, but it is also an opportunity for administrators to sell the qualities of their school and excite the candidates with regard to becoming a part of your instructional team. Many districts have put incentive plans into place to recruit teachers to come and stay in lower performing schools; however, the success of these programs has been disappointing. In Florida, some school districts ranked teachers from across the district according to performance and sent the highest performing teachers to the lowest performing schools with a bonus for "taking the challenge." Before the end of the year, many of those teachers had resigned or requested to return the money and go back to their schools. In short, they were unable to get the same results in the new environment and money was not enough of a motivator to solidify success in the challenged school. This doesn't mean they were very poor teachers. These teachers had proven to get results in less challenged environments. They simply validated the thought that success in one environment doesn't automatically result in success in another.

Celebrating Your Team

Showing improvement in student achievement, even small changes along the way, is also an important aspect of creating your new majority. When teachers see that their hard work in the classroom is paying off, it is a great motivator and cause for celebration. Take time to point out when difficult subgroups show gains, attendance rates improve, grade levels or teams of teachers have perfect attendance, and when disciplinary infractions or other targeted concerns are reduced. The more we point out the small things, the more staff members begin to take pride in their accomplishments. This builds confidence and encourages them to continue putting forth effort to improve themselves and others. Showing and celebrating success demonstrates to staff members that their efforts are not in vain and that we recognize the impact they are making on our students and our school. Recognition and reward for a job well done may be leadership's most effective but underused tool. There is an abundance of research on this that has been overlooked for long enough (Schmoker, 2001).

Big Steps, Big Motivators

"Changing too much, too quickly may cause damage or leave valuable things behind. For any organization to progress in a healthy way, there must be careful balancing of the wisdom of the past and the needs for the future."

—Woodrow Hughes

When starting at a new school, many principals are over-aggressive toward attempting to fix all of the school's problems in the first year. The next step toward creating a positive majority in your new school is to focus on relationships; build relationships with your staff and work toward being supportive. Most teachers really want to be successful in their classrooms, enjoy coming to school every day, and want to feel like they belong and are respected by their colleagues. *I am convinced that no teacher wakes up and says, "I want to fail students today by providing them a horrible educational experience" just as I'm sure no parent says, "I want my child to be a horrible student and fail miserably in school."*

Michael Fullan found that **"most people want to be part of their organization; they want to know the organization's purpose, they want to make a difference"** (Fullan, 2001, p. 52). A simple way to begin building relationships is to get out of the office and get to know the people in your building.

Sustaining Your New Majority

It's all too easy, and common, for leaders to build the new majority but not continue with the work required to sustain it. The following list is by no means complete, but it provides a starting point from which you can continue to work as a cohesive unit.

- Build genuine relationships with students, staff and parents.
- Support teachers at all times in regard to parent and student behavior.
- Do not try to make big, sweeping changes right away.
- Support your staff. Never make a staff member feel like she did the wrong thing by informing you of a concern.
- Be thorough. Check things out. Do not punish a student unless you are absolutely sure the student's behavior was inappropriate.
- Encourage your staff to let you know how you can help them with classroom issues.
- Don't expect the teacher to investigate the issue; they need to focus on instruction.
- Let your bus drivers know you are there to support them.
- Be visible in the cafeteria and the hallways. Spend time with your students at lunch and during passing times.
- Discuss student consequences with the staff member involved and ask for their opinion.
- Value teacher's opinions and support their important work in the classroom.
- Hold everyone accountable and to the same standard.
- Celebrate small victories along the way to your goals.
- Hire people who fit.
- Involve your staff—they may know more than you do.
- Collaborate with teachers in decision-making.
- Make your school a fun place for all.

Productive Professional Development

One of the keys to creating a new positive majority is to provide staff with informative, effective and relevant professional development. To improve student achievement, schools must arm their teachers with the best instructional methods and materials available. I am ashamed to admit that as a new principal, I frequently initiated staff development sessions for the faculty after school, and then, unobtrusively, tiptoed out of the back of the room and returned to my office to attend to "more important things." Thinking back on it, I see what an inappropriate message I was sending: "Learning is for other people; I had more important things to do." This quickly changed! The principal who *joins with* the faculty and students in learning activities is the one who changes the school culture into one that is hospitable to lifelong learning (DuFour, Eaker & DuFour, 2005).

Quite often, when we are called in to speak to schools and school districts, we will be introduced by an administrator who subsequently sneaks to the back of the room and out the door after a few minutes of the presentation. Although I understand that administrators are busy and are pulled in many directions, this sends the message to the others in the room that professional development is not important. When teachers see that the professional development is not important to their leader, it becomes unimportant to them. It is our belief that administrators who are trying to build a strong culture should not schedule professional development if they are not going to be active participants. This is the perfect opportunity for administrators to show teachers that you are committed to learning new things and are growing your resources along with them.

Additionally, how does a principal answer follow-up questions if he or she did not see and engage in the presentation? This sends a more damaging message when district or state leaders sit in professional development sessions and work on their computers, tablets or smart phones totally unengaged in the training. Participating in professional development sessions together is part of the lifelong learning partnership that leaders, at all levels, must engage in with their staff if they desire to build commitment.

Some Additional Tips to Achieve Your New Majority

I have been in schools that faced seemingly insurmountable challenges where teachers and students were happy and working hard, the climate was great, and improvement was slow but on the horizon. Despite the odds, there was momentum and people enjoyed coming to this place to work and learn. I would love to tell that my leadership alone made this possible; however, I know that my team's dedication to making school a great place set the tone for our success. I am not naive in that I clearly understand that I am not solely responsible for teacher morale but that teachers also impact the morale of the school by their behaviors, beliefs, actions and relationships. When building a new majority this is something you must understand and prepare for as a leader.

There are situations where, no matter what you do, some people will remain outliers. Don't allow this to discourage or derail your mission. I remember being in a school where I personally purchased birthday cards and $5 gift cards to Starbucks or McDonald's for staff birthdays. I would take a day during the summer and personalize each person's birthday card and file them by month. My wonderful secretaries, Mrs. Bailey and Mrs. Dawson, would make sure that I got the gift cards in their mailboxes on the night before their big day so they would have them when they arrived at work. Additionally, I would recognize them with a birthday cake during our monthly celebration and make a huge deal of their contribution to our school. One day after a celebration, I received a call from the teacher's union about a teacher who didn't want a Starbucks card because a peer had received a McDonald's card the month before. I chuckled and moved forward as I understood that there will always be someone in every crowd who will never be satisfied.

Below is a short list of little things leaders can do to make their school a fun place. Visit www.beyondtheoryedu.com to find a more inclusive list of ideas to help you make your school environment one where teachers never want to leave.

- Visit the classrooms and leave a note or treat.
- Interact with your students and staff, and let them know that you genuinely care.
- Open up your soda machine at lunch or after school.
- On the night before the first day, when your staff is gone, leave a "first-day gift" on their desks.
- Buy a George Foreman electric grill and BBQ for your staff in the lounge.
- Solve a big problem.
- Send out an email that says "Free Subs!" Take time to "sub" for your teachers for 30 minutes for the first three people who respond to your email.

Cylinder 7: Implementing a Year-Long Success Program

"This is a work in progress. It has to be monitored—both its details and the implementation of the details."

—Gary Wadler

Without constant monitoring, the Continual Improvement Plan and the processes put in place can quickly lose momentum. Educators are dealing with a myriad of mandates and day-to-day problems making it easy to get off track. When we start a school year it appears the end is so far away. Before we know it, we are celebrating the winter holidays, planning end of the year activities and looking back wondering where did the time go? Implementation and monitoring of a year-long program is not always an easy task; however, it is an essential responsibility of the principal and staff in the continual improvement plan. When making critical, data-driven decisions as part of a continual improvement plan, it is imperative that everyone is doing their part to ensure the plan is implemented with fidelity and that we are getting results. The information provided prior to this chapter offers methods that serve as the foundation for a flawless implementation of a CIP. In this chapter we will discuss the implementation of the CIP and the importance of monitoring the data and processes in place to maintain momentum throughout the entire school year.

The CIP is developed to provide a clear purpose for our work and ensure we have an established method for identifying support services, methods of instructional delivery, diagnostic materials, enrichment/intervention strategies, and evaluating the empirically sound year-long process. The CIP and the entire process of teaching and learning must be led by the principal, who is the instructional leader, and supported by other instructional leaders, teachers, and district staff.

Instructional leaders must play an active role and motivate others to stay engaged in the improvement plan when implementing a year-long program. This means there must be planned momentum checks and boosters to keep the train moving in the event that your engine starts to lose steam. Leaders get these results by staying encouraged and assisting in developing the CIP, assisting teachers and others in completing intervention notebooks, observing intervention integration in classrooms, providing samples and modeling differentiating curriculum, providing timely feedback, responding to data, and celebrating small as well as large victories.

How Three Schools Implemented a Year-Long Success Program that Worked

Scott's Thoughts

I must begin by using a quote from Michael Schmoker, **"You must begin early . . . get the data in front of your staff, evaluate the data and create goals based upon that data"**

(HOPE Foundation, 2002). During my last nine years at Crestwood, we had high student performance data. One of the reasons for this success was the way we analyzed our data. We got the data in front of the staff early and used our data to drive our instruction.

Navigating Your Plan, Without Getting Lost

Years ago, I had a speaking engagement in Austin, Texas, and I had an early morning flight for my return to St. Louis. Well, I am getting old, and my eyes do not work as well as they used to. When I got in my car and looked at the printout of my downloaded directions, I realized that I could not read the directions. The font was too small, my eyes were not quite awake, and the lighting was far from optimal. As I took one wrong turn after another, I realized I was not going to make my flight. I was so frustrated that I almost missed the huge "airport" sign. One of the first stops I made when I returned to St. Louis was at the cell phone store. I needed a new phone, with a GPS. Now, wherever I need to go, I just enter my destination, and my GPS guides me with clear precision to where I need to go.

Whether you know it or not, there is a GPS in each of our schools. Our GPS is our data. When I make a wrong turn in my car, my GPS does not say, "You idiot, you made a wrong turn." Instead, it says in that kind and mechanical tone, "recalculating route." The first thing a GPS tries to do is find you an alternate route to get you to your destination. Perhaps you will need to drive a few blocks before turning left, to get back on track. Or maybe you need to make a "U-turn" or start over with a completely new route. When I was a principal, the data guided our journey. Throughout the year, we met in our grade-level teams and looked at our "GPS" to see if we were still on track, or if we needed to "recalculate" our route. Using our data helped us create our year-long program.

"Even if you are on the right track, you'll get run over if you just sit there."

—Will Rogers

The key to navigating your year-long program is to create goals. These can be wide-sweeping building goals or grade-level SMART Goals. At Crestwood, each grade level or department (art, music, PE, remedial reading, etc.) created a SMART goal (see Cylinder Two). Our Student Achievement, Professional Development and Character committees also created these goals. During the year, each committee provided reports at our staff meetings in regard to progress they made toward meeting their goals. Our grade-level teams also reported on their goals during our monthly grade-level data meetings. The "bottom line" goal for everyone at Crestwood Elementary was improving student achievement. Our Character Committee focused on improving our student character, which translated into improved classroom cultures and led to higher student achievement. Our Professional Development Committee focused on providing high-quality learning opportunities for staff, which led to improved instructional skills and improved student achievement.

In order to ensure building-wide improvement, it is important to help one student at a time. Many schools do not focus on individual students. At Crestwood, many of our teachers used student portfolios in their classrooms to stay focused on individual students' progress and ability levels. It has been suggested that a portfolio is like a color video with sound, much more vivid than just a test paper (Stiggins, 1994). It gives a fuller picture and provides supportive evidence to substantiate the feedback or grade that has been given. When I consult with schools and school districts, one of my key messages is to focus on every single student. Once I had an administrator say to me, "There are students that walk across the stage at the eighth-grade graduation who I have never seen before." I find that very sad! Eighth-grade graduation is the culmination of three years of work and relationship-building. For a principal to not know his or her students after three years is disappointing. Improving student achievement takes the entire staff working together and a principal must be involved in these meetings about individual students.

When we had grade-level meetings at Crestwood, I was an active participant as the classroom teacher and others shared information about each student. The ELL teacher might share how a student was doing with regard to improving his vocabulary. The reading teacher may discuss how another student was growing in her fluency. The developmental math teacher may share that a student had finally mastered double-digit addition, and the principal might discuss details with regard to a home problem that a student was having. It takes all of us, working together, discussing students' strengths and weaknesses to truly impact student achievement. If the principal does not know the student, he/she cannot be an active participant in the conversation.

We all have students who move away from our school. On occasion, months later, I have run into principals of schools where some of my former students have enrolled. Often, I will ask the other principal how my former student is doing in their school. It is *alarming* to me when time after time the principal says that they do not even know the student. Please understand that I know that this can't be the expectation in a larger school, but in a typically sized elementary school (400-600 students) principals need to get to know your students! Learn their names. Find out their hobbies! Who plays soccer? Who is a girl scout? Who takes piano lessons? Whose dad is in jail? All of these situations can deeply impact a student's education.

Training for Testing

In Cylinder 5, we discussed Intervention Notebooks. Each month during these student meetings, data and notes should be collected. In October, if you notice that Larry is struggling in math, find an intervention or strategy to help him with math in October, not March. **"For students to succeed, they need to believe that they can learn and that what they are learning is useful, relevant and meaningful for them. They need to know that they belong in the classroom and that they are responsible for their own learning, as well as their own**

behavior" (Gregory & Chapman, 2002, p.1). The key to Schmoker's quote about evaluating data and creating goals is to get started early. March is too late to get excited about improving student achievement; however, March isn't too late to put an intervention strategy into place. March was "No-Interruption Month" at Crestwood. No interruptions meant no field trips and no assemblies during the month before state testing. Time was protected for instructional purposes. During March, students needed to be taking part in practice-test scenarios. If students walk into class in April and all of a sudden they have to sit at their desk for three or four hours a day testing, they need to be ready. Training students in "test-like" situations will help them be successful. This is similar to running a marathon. You do not just show up at the race without training. You work for months and months, getting into the best shape possible to run the race. With state achievement tests, you do the same thing. You start in August and work diligently on concepts for months to prepare for the big event in April.

Before you start working on your year-long goals, make sure you have a plan in place for keeping the morale high in your building. We have shared many ways to motivate staff throughout this book, but the most important motivation is being a good leader; supporting your teachers when they need your help and listening to teachers when they need your ear. I have had conversations with principals who start off the year with guns blazing. The start of the year is refreshing and the opening staff meeting is full of energy and excitement. The first few weeks of school run smoothly, but then it hits. It can happen during the first semester or even the first month. The leader, so full of energy and inspiration, has a bad day and fails to handle a situation well. Teachers start to feel unsupported and that beginning-of-the-year excitement starts to falter. When you get busy, keep your staff focused on the building goals. However, do not overwhelm or overwork your staff. If you sense stress and burnout due to turning in grades, excessive meetings, etc., give your staff a break. There were months when I canceled or postponed a staff meeting or grade-level meetings. During April, when we were MAP testing, we did not have a staff meeting or grade-level meetings. When you give your staff a break, they appreciate it very much and it gives them an opportunity to refresh.

"Teachers who educate children deserve more honor than parents who merely gave them birth; for bare life is furnished by one, the other ensures a good life."

—Aristotle

Many years ago, we had the chance to purchase some used executive chairs for our building. As I went from class to class, I was so impressed with my teachers. One after another their responses were: "Mr. Taylor, I certainly don't need a new chair. I never have time to sit down." Now, that is a perfect response! Quite often, when I visit schools, I see teachers sitting behind their desks more often than I see them actively engaging with students. However, our teachers were so engaged in teaching and learning that they did not have time to sit down.

"Modern cynics and skeptics . . . see no harm in paying those to whom we entrust the minds of their children a smaller wage than is paid to those to whom they entrust the care of their plumbing."

—John F. Kennedy

We worked on creating building goals for years and each year we gradually improved our process. Years ago, I always put building goal teams at the end of our staff meeting agenda. There would be at least two or three meetings each year during which we would run out of time and would not have time for our goal teams to report to the staff. Teachers told me that they did not feel our goal teams were accomplishing as much as they should due to the lack of accountability and reduced opportunity for sharing their progress at staff meetings. As a result of those conversations, we changed our agendas and moved our goal team items to the first half of the meeting.

"The work will wait while you show your child the rainbow, but the rainbow won't wait while you do the work!"

—Patricia Clifford

Ty's Take: Being SMART

Implementation at my school was an enlightening process that will serve as a great example for leaders struggling to bring about change in both the school and the community. Working as a PLC, my staff and I developed a school improvement plan based on trend data and other non-academic factors that appeared to have an impact on our school environment. As a school-based team we gathered and used our performance data to establish school-wide SMART goals that aligned with our district's goals.

After reviewing the data and establishing school-wide targets, the teachers jumped right in to determine what they needed to do as a grade-level to change their outcome. The grade-level PLCs developed grade-level and classroom goals that were aligned to school-wide goals and designed to improve their performance.

Students who had not met grade-level goals prior to the start of school were placed on an intensive acceleration plan while intervention notebooks were being developed and their performance was monitored consistently as part of their intervention. We worked collaboratively to select sound interventions that would address every level of need and ensure that every child's need was addressed through an intervention included in our list of available improvement options. Figure 14 provides a visual to illustrate our focus.

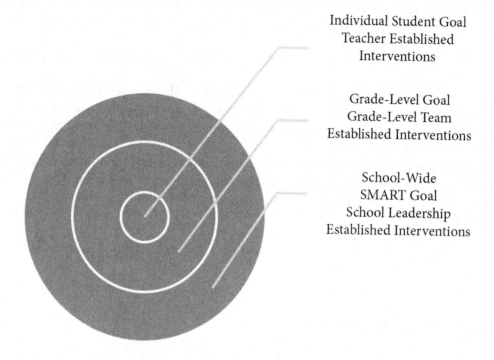

Individual Student Goal
Teacher Established
Interventions

Grade-Level Goal
Grade-Level Team
Established Interventions

School-Wide
SMART Goal
School Leadership
Established Interventions

Figure 14: Targeted Interventions

My Title I teacher, Brenda Daniels, explained this differentiated approach to interventions in a remarkable way at a parent meeting. When asked about the various intervention plans, she shared, **"Some students need maintenance like a yearly physical, some need assistance for a symptom, similar to a common cold or flu, while others need intensive interventions because of the severity of their condition, such as a patient with cancer."**

Teachers updated intervention notebooks throughout the year as student performance was assessed and shifts in learning occurred. They used these notebooks as a means of documenting their efforts, tracking student progress, and acknowledging and addressing student misunderstandings of academic vocabulary and content. Designated intervention teachers were responsible for documenting individualized enrichment, maintenance or remediation interventions. The tracking system we developed and utilized was a great resource.

Interventions within the school took place in the classrooms, library, computer lab, pull-out Title I classrooms, Special Education classrooms and unified arts classrooms. All teachers at some point within the school day were involved in providing students with either enrichment, maintenance or remediation work. We believed in the old saying, "divide and conquer," in an effort to raise student achievement. Interventions within the building were provided and documented by the intervention teacher and listed in the intervention notebook by the regular education classroom teacher, who was responsible for monitoring interventions. Accountability became everyone's responsibility. We left no rock unturned!

It was evident that change was needed as the staff and I were spending an inordinate amount of time dealing with inappropriate student behavior. Knowing that without a learning climate that supports teaching and learning, improvements in other areas would be difficult to achieve. Student discipline quickly became the focal point of our plan to improve student achievement. Other areas built into our plan were student attendance, student academics, principal as instructional leader, and enhanced teaching qualities.

A Culturally Based Discipline Plan

After discussing school dynamics with co-author, Dr. Catherine Barnes, I decided to look into a resource she suggested that dealt with cultural audits and culturally sensitive approaches to leadership and discipline. She talked extensively about the work she was doing around cultural competency with the Jacksonville Alliance of Black School Educators (JABSE) and the MODELS Equity Project through the University of Florida's Lastinger Foundation. This helped us to audit the impact our personal thoughts and beliefs have on how we deal with culture in our schools. I remember her sharing that "our lack of understanding breeds fear that is often the cause of actions that we, when asked, often can't explain." Based on our discussions, newly discovered factors impacting my school, and readings on the culture of the students we serve, the staff and I created a "Culturally Based Discipline System;" A system that taught students desired behaviors as opposed to being strictly punitive in nature. A system that defined, modeled and was built on mutual respect and making good decisions. This new program required a new process and limited situations that enhanced inappropriate behaviors while it encouraged redirection and discouraged exclusion of students as a disciplinary option.

The Individual Guided Staff Development (IGSD) action research started with me addressing where student misconduct took place using student discipline data. What were the antecedents that led to these conflicts? Using teacher referrals and student written explanations of situations, we audited discipline data by having kids, in a later conversation, answer the following questions:

1. What happened?
2. What could you have done differently in this situation?
3. What would your parent say about your behavior?
4. What will you do differently next time based on this discussion?

These questions were based on the Concerns Based Adoption Model (CBAM) developed by Gene Hall and Shirley Hord (Hall & Hord, 2001). Students helped by providing insight and often provided information needed to build strong systems and address other concerns.

After reviewing the data, it was observed that most of the student misconduct occurred in non-instructional areas (hallways, lunch, recess, breakfast, bathrooms, etc.) and spilled over into the classrooms. My first thoughts were to address these concerns with students at the beginning of the year, but I still needed to understand what it was about these situations that led to the conflict. So I called on some students and staff members and asked them some critical questions.

Many of our teachers were not maintaining or tracking nonacademic data during the school year, thus it was easy to understand why there was no information on specific student infractions. Most did not have a clear explanation for the conflicts that were taking place or any empirical data that would help narrow the incidents to a specific time or place. Students, on the other hand, were a much better source of information. They were able, despite the "no snitching" code, to provide a clear understanding of the problems and how they occurred. Information from students was collected and analyzed for thematic, institutional, or systemic concerns and possible solutions were solicited and recorded.

The very candid and unfiltered information the students shared indicated and validated information that the administration had collected in the audit of the student misconduct referrals. Students stated that there were common areas and times of the day that needed attention. These areas and times included:

1. before school outside playtime;
2. student breakfast;
3. hallway transitions to and from classes;
4. beginning of homeroom/classroom;
5. lunchroom;
6. recess time;
7. restroom time; and
8. dismissal time.

Because academic and nonacademic data has an impact on school culture, climate and teacher and student performance, we created a report to validate this information and presented it to the staff. We had gathered together to address these issues as part of our school's Continual Improvement Plan (CIP) for the upcoming school year.

One area that was not addressed in the CIP, but was a critical part of dealing with discipline as well as student achievement and quality teaching, was the concept of "Management by

Walking Around," as articulated by Edward Deming et al in the Total Quality Management (TQM) process. Ensuring that all administrators and school leaders understood that being out of the office and in the school was an expectation became a high priority. Our increased presence encouraged effective behaviors by students and staff alike. This allowed the instructional leaders to have a first-hand view of what was occurring in all parts of the school and in relation to the effective implementation of the CIP.

Within a few weeks, staff and students became accustomed to the principal being around the building and within classrooms. If multiple regressions had been applied to factors that fostered and or improved student behavior and enhanced teaching quality, "Management by Walking Around" would have appeared to be significant.

The Seminar Process

The "Seminar" process was tied directly into the Positive Behavioral Support (PBS) intervention program. Simply speaking, the seminar process involves students and staff gathering together and discussing school issues. A component of the previous year's CIP was to train select staff members using the PBS program. We utilized this training to implement new interventions and showcase teachers who participated the year before. According to Kate Thiry of Dublin City Schools, "PBS is a school-wide program designed to respond immediately to positive and negative behaviors. In the PBS model, students were taught replacement behaviors that were consistent among all staff members and reinforced expected behaviors. The PBS model maximizes instructional time on task by minimizing student discipline problems" (Dublin Literacy Conference, 2006).

It took several weeks to observe a difference in student behavior. After about six weeks, the entire student body was able to recite the school-wide procedures and expectations that had greatly decreased student misconduct. Observers of the "Seminar" process had commented that the process should be a standard component of every school that has discipline concerns. Parents commented on the fact that this process supported the concept of learning replacement behaviors and placed an emphasis on shared responsibility and accountability between the student, parent and the school.

Triangle of Academic Success:

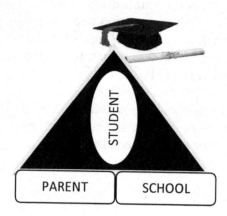

Figure 15: Triangle of Academic Success

Co-author Dr. Catherine Barnes refers to Figure 15, as the Triangle of Academic Success (TAS) Model. Her model defines an educational partnership and outlines the roles each partner must play to ensure that students, parents and teachers get what is desired from every academic encounter. It suggests the novel premise that schools are not solely responsible for how kids turn out and how successful they are but that parents, students and the school share responsibility; and that when either party is not doing their part then success is more challenging, failure is often plausible and none of the parties involved experience academic or social success. Every entity has a responsibility in student success and the partnership is designed to help everyone understand what they can do to support the process.

The model provides a framework that outlines and defines the role and responsibilities of the parent, school and the student in ensuring academic and social success (Figure 16). Because research indicates parental engagement declines as the student progresses throughout school and the role parents play often shifts from active participator to "on-call" interventionist at best in many instances, the need to outline long-term partnership expectations is critical. The model suggests a few basic behaviors that impact student success but schools should modify to accommodate grade, course or school specific needs.

Parent	Student	School
Know the school calendar, including progress report and report card dates.	Communicate openly with your parents about school and invite them to school events.	Commit to engaging parents and students as partners in success.
Review report cards and progress reports and make immediate contact with specific teachers when progress starts to decline.	Ask for help when you need it. Even if you must do it through email, text, by leaving a note or on your exit tickets.	Develop a communication plan and follow it. Avoid last minute notifications when possible.
Ensure students attend school regularly and on time. No free days.	Attend school daily, and go to every class. ON TIME.	Establish a partnership culture. Hold staff accountable for maintaining a welcoming environment.
Ask daily, what did you learn today? By subject or class. Ex. What did you learn in math today? Show me what you completed or give me an example. Do not allow answers like nothing or I don't know. Probe or contact the teacher immediately.	Find clever ways to avoid conflict. If you know something is going to happen, tell your parents or school officials IMMEDIATELY so that they can address it and keep you out of it.	Develop systems that allow all parents opportunities to contribute and be an active partner in the school. If a parent can't read to students during the day offer opportunities to grill hotdogs on his/her day off for a teacher or student celebration.
Go to the school campus, at least quarterly, to review student progress and interact with staff.	Study every day. If you have nothing to do, then read a magazine, story on the internet, or watch a video to help with another subject.	Be sensitive to educational levels, experiences, work schedules, when planning events and meetings. Try meeting in the community on a Saturday instead of at noon on Tuesday.
Maintain strong, positive relationships with school staff.	Set aside time for homework. Encourage your friends to do so as well.	Involve ALL students and parents in decisions. Sometimes the "good" kids are the ones who see nothing wrong or are comfortable with the status quo.
Presume positive intensions and support the school's rules and processes.	Commit to paying attention when in class. Use hallway time and lunch for socializing but make sure you make it to class on time.	Hold everyone accountable, including school personnel, for maintaining good relationships and keeping the partnership at the center of decisions.

Parent	Student	School
Volunteer. This is a buzz word that turns people off because of time and the feeling that you can not help. WRONG—you can give an hour to prepare flyers for mail outs, find resources like gift certificates when at your favorite restaurant, buy a case of water for an event, take tickets at a production, help in the media center, help with a weekend project, and much more. There are many ways to help without taking a lot of time away from work, or without interacting directly with students.	Take information sent home for your parents to them. Do not determine what they need or do not need. Sometimes, they find things important that you think are no big deal. Remember they are your partner and should have information to make decisions that support you and the school.	Select, use, and require teachers to use culturally sensitive, relevant, and rigorous materials daily. Plan lessons and other student centered materials or activities around student, parent, and school data. Commit to moving outside of the cookie-cutter approaches that exclude or otherwise hinder performance and participation.
Have adult conversations with the adults in the school. Contain emotions and always speak positively about the school, teachers, and students in the presence of students.	Get involved in clubs, sports, and campus projects. This helps you to connect to the school.	Be responsible in your reporting—gather all facts and address needs in a timely manner. Remember, you are a partner and failure of either part of the equation is failure for all.
Speak and share information as a partner of the school. Avoid putting the school, staff, or student down.	Follow rules so that your parents and teachers do not have to take time away from your goals to address things you already know.	Be creative and supportive of the dynamics in your school and in every classroom. Monitor and address people and processes that hinder or do not support the mission.
Always approach problems as a partner. How can "we" fix the issue so "WE" are successful?	Eat and drink healthy stuff and get rest. It sounds corny but it really does matter. You think and feel better. Enjoy your junk food but know it could make acne, weight, and energy a distractor.	Listen to the other partners and know when things should change. Work with them and always be honest about what can and cannot be done. Look for win-wins and at the very least, seek consensus.

Parent	Student	School
Speak positively about education and set high expectations for student performance. Talk about college, passing ACT and SAT, and other post-secondary topics at every grade level. It is never too early. Do virtual college tours, talk about possible careers and what it takes to get there, daily. Remember preparing to be "smart" and to have a future starts NOW.	Be the best YOU that YOU can be. Start your own style if you can't afford someone else's.	Create a safe, equitable, and rigorous environment that allows you and all partners to reach your goal of overall success. Share the responsibility and allow them to be the expert on the role they play. Remember it is a partnership and ideas should flow both ways.
Close all gaps in communication. Never respond without hearing from all partners first. If something doesn't sound right, check it out. Be nosey, check planners and backpacks, and look at who your kids hang out with. It isn't always the kids around your child that are the problem but the synergy created when they are together.	Be respectful and try your best. The term "respect" means so many different things so always try to stick to the basics— No cursing, talking back or interrupting when an adult is talking, listen, follow rules, speak kindly and be nice. If you are angry, take a moment to get your emotions under control before speaking, keep your hands and inappropriate thoughts to yourself, do what you are asked—when asked, be helpful, and try your best, speak the way you want to be spoken to, and when you have an issue, seek help from one of your partners (parents or at school)—don't try to fix adults. You have adult partners to help you with other adults.	Do not, and do not permit others to attack or put down your partners. Ever. Remember you must support them and ensure their image is safe. You are their advocate in and out of the school. They are your family. Treat them that way.

Parent	Student	School
Address issues immediately with the student and school. Remember, you are a partner, not the enemy, so even when things seem like they are not right, check it out and look for solutions, not war. You are on the same team. Be honest and admit when you need help, feel excluded, or want to be more involved.	Dare to make school the new cool. Take the lead on asking questions and working hard to get good grades. Talk about college, passing ACT and SAT, and other post-secondary topics with your friends. Remember, preparing and studying wins over "smart" every time.	Be fair and consistent. Apply rules, policies, and processes consistently so that there is a standard that everyone can count on. Be honest and admit when you are wrong. As partners everyone must be able to trust what is being said. Remember, you are a partner, not the enemy, so even when things seem like they are not right, check it out and look for solutions, not war. You are on the same team.
Approach all problems with solutions or potential solutions.	Approach all problems with solutions or potential solutions.	Approach all problems with solutions or potential solutions.
Remove and do not allow excuses for poor performance with either partner. Use progress toward goals as an indicator of your success and that of the other partners (student and school).	You have adult partners to help you address issues—use them. Their experiences may save you some trouble.	Give students the best education possible. Staff must be accountable for student academic reviews, monitoring, planning, and providing the best educational opportunity possible.
Enforce all rules consistently. If the school has a policy, hold students accountable for following it. Do not make excuses.	Ask for help when you need it and how you can help when you don't need help. SET, TRACK, and REACH both short and long term goals for success. Even kindergartners can set goals for their week, month, and after high school.	Build relationships, partnerships, and know your kids and parents. Do your homework and focus on what is important for the success of your partnership at all times.

Parent	Student	School
Provide a designated place and time for homework. This time should be free from duties such as watching siblings, chores, etc. Keep the school informed about external factors that may impact the success of student and school efforts. (*e.g. Death, illness, divorce, etc.*)	Use timelines and set deadlines. Use a planner. You are young and smart now so this will prepare you for when you are old like your partners (parents and school personnel).	Practice effective communication and make yourself available. PLAN, PLAN, and PLAN again to be sure you get information to the other partners in a timely manner. Everyone cannot do last minute or adjust to poor planning.
Remove external distractions and have students make timelines and both of you track progress on projects, exams, etc.	Take notes on everything and use them to study. If you need help figuring out what is important, ask. This also helps you share things with your parents and proves you are listening.	Require all parties involved in the school to value EVERY parent and student. Make it the standard way of work and do not settle for less.
Establish email and phone expectations for school staff and use this to gather information, offer assistance, and support the partnership.	Track your own progress. If you see you are getting behind, get busy fixing it now. DO ALL OF YOUR WORK. No matter how useless it may seem. If it is busy work-turn it into an easy grade.	Be on time and always honor the partnership. Do your best to hire, maintain, and train quality staff and put systems in place to ensure your responsibilities are met.
Maintain open communication with the school about ALL issues. Listen out for hot topics that your kids talk about with friends and make the school aware—IMMEDIATELY. Remember you are a PARTNER and the school's issue is your issue.	Remember you are a PARTNER and the school's issues are your issues. Do your part and hold your partners responsible for doing theirs as well. The term "snitch" is one associated with irresponsible behaviors. Find a way to share things that could keep you and others out of trouble and safe. Protect your image.	Remember you are a PARTNER and the school's issue is your issue. Respect what everyone brings to the table. Respond to concerns quickly and value them as much as you want to be valued. Be professional and respectful. Our high horse is a pony in many situations. Be comfortable allowing everyone to display their strengths.

Figure 16: Outline of Roles and Responsibilities

Incorporating Cathy's model within our school reduced the "Got ya" effect of discipline. We administered a survey and found that students and parents felt more informed of the school procedures, expectations, policies, routines and rules and believed they were an integral part of the school's success. Additionally, staff members acknowledged that this strategy had garnered many benefits not initially considered when "Seminar" was first designed and implemented. Such benefits included a ten-minute per day before school reading/homework program that yielded an additional 30 hours a year in student engagement. Other benefits included a review of the school day agenda, morning announcements and heading off behavioral concerns before the start of the school day.

Positive Behavioral Supports

As my school staff received training in PBS, we recognized the process we had chosen to improve our school climate would work only if everyone was consistent in following the school-wide procedures and enforcing school-wide consequences. As an outcome of the PBS training and successes in addressing earlier concerns, select staff members believed that we could work on other discipline concerns as part of the continual improvement cycle. The next concern to be addressed as a component of student misbehavior was to reduce bus referrals. Staff members provided a role-playing simulation to model and teach students how to appropriately ride the school bus to and from school. In classrooms, teachers asked students to provide examples of appropriate behavior on a school bus. Students shared appropriate behaviors of what would be heard and witnessed on a bus, as homeroom teachers listed their responses. Their responses became the procedures that all students were then to follow and abide by.

As part of the plan, we noticed many benefits from the implementation of the school's PBS climate improvement program. Listed below are procedures used in implementing, monitoring and revising the program to improve discipline and to improve the other non-academic components of the reform model (i.e. instructional leadership, attendance, achievement, and teaching quality):

1. Identification of a data-based area of need.
2. Developing a plan with staff members to address the needs.
3. Implementation of the program(s) determined to be most effective.
4. Assessment of whether or not the implementation has met the need.
5. Start the change process all over in order to improve the effort, if needed.

Preliminary student discipline data indicated that the programs implemented had partially been a success. Attendance had increased to 95% compared to prior years of 93%; out-of-school suspensions had decreased to 142 compared to more than 248 suspensions in the prior school year; and student achievement had increased when looking at 3rd Grade October Ohio

Achievement Test (OAT) data where students scored 40% in the current year, compared with scores of 22% and 23% in prior years.

Cathy's Commentary: A Secondary Intervention Model That Worked

Secondary schools often face challenges our elementary counterparts find impossible to imagine so we thought it was important to include a secondary intervention method that was used to improve student performance. Working with a tremendous team of teachers and administrators, we began by reviewing our data and determined that many of our after school, before school, and weekend efforts were not well attended and that we had to capture our students during the school day if we were to truly provide them with intervention services. We looked for a way to incorporate our intervention method into our school day since the majority of our students were either bus riders or had responsibilities that made it impossible for them to come early or stay after school.

We established school-wide targets based on our data. Our targets aligned with our district's targets and were used to create a sense of urgency in our students and staff. That data was then broken down into grade levels and grade-level goals were quickly and strategically established. Within the grade-level PLCs, teachers targeted students and identified which classroom interventions would best support their learning process. Teachers then divided class time to ensure everyone was focusing on targeted skills based on the needs of the students they served.

We implemented a school-wide plan which included a timeline for common assignments, assessments, and the inclusion of targeted opening lessons presented daily as part of the regular lesson structure. These mini-lessons were based on recent, relevant assessment data and were a part of the school-wide, grade-level, subject-specific intervention calendar.

Grade-level administrators, along with lead teachers, developed the intervention calendar on a monthly basis to ensure students were getting an opportunity to practice key skills. Teachers, using their monitoring system, would measure and document student progress to determine what needed to be incorporated in the regular lesson or what needed to be the focus in small-group instructional sessions.

Additionally, we designed a modified instructional schedule where students would return to their designated enrichment classroom, every Wednesday for 90 minutes of targeted intervention services. During this time, teachers provided direct instruction and/or computer or small-group intervention services based on each student's identified need. The period was divided so that teachers would address grade-level deficits and individual student deficits within the 90-minute time frame. This shift required teachers to be fully committed to moving students forward and to understand the importance of the intervention.

One of the biggest challenges was getting the few skeptics to understand they were not losing instructional time but were gaining remediation time within the school day to target specific student needs. The other challenge was the teachers' comfort with the content they were required to share during these intervention periods. Because of the number of students needing specific support, all teachers had to be involved and were often facilitating lessons that were outside of their comfort zone. After a few failed sessions, we had to ease the stress on the teachers facilitating sessions as well as those teachers who worried about their colleagues inadvertently giving students the wrong information. We solicited teachers to provide the instruction via video. This was a big hit. Grade-level, content-specific lessons were developed, with examples, and viewed in classes throughout the school. These lessons were made available for teachers to show during the first few minutes of the intervention period. Teachers would show the video, guide students through the examples as they were being presented, provide students with problems to complete, use the answer key provided to check student's answers, and then forward any questions to the student's content area teacher for further explanation.

We used this structure throughout the year and, despite the initial start-up challenges discussed, we were proud of our results. We were able to give short assessments during the intervention time, get students accustomed to taking assessments in the same environment and format as the state assessment and provide immediate feedback prior to any misconception becoming an unproductive academic habit.

After working through the kinks, teachers enjoyed having the time set aside to focus on what they knew were deficiencies. It was empowering and significantly improved the way teachers and students performed. This process also helped teachers and students to develop productive and meaningful relationships which research supports as a significant key to improved performance.

Cylinder 8: Measuring Your Results and Celebrating Successes

"The ancient Romans had a tradition: whenever one of their engineers constructed an arch, as the capstone was hoisted into place, the engineer assumed accountability for his work in the most profound way possible: he stood under the arch."

—Michael Armstrong

Too often, schools implement strategies for improvement, yet fail to properly measure their results. Spending time on new policies, procedures, and planning techniques that don't work would be wasting time. Much like student learning, we need to track results and make data-based decisions regarding our program of change; we need to know exactly what is working, what needs to be improved, and what needs to be stopped immediately. The Eight Cylinder Reform Model is perpetual! Too often, processes do not continue as shifts and trends are recognized. Remember, any one can collect the data. The power of data, however, is its use. Many schools are data rich, yet information poor limiting it's impact on student achievement.

Measuring results and celebrating success are major components of the ECRM, serving as the catalyst (or fuel) for the next phase of the improvement plan. Data will drive the course of determining the overall success of previously implemented interventions. We must determine which components of our CIP are to be continued and which need to be abandoned; we must work collaboratively to determine if any new components are required. Subsequently, conclusions must be drawn about efforts and progress toward meeting goals.

In essence, we measure results by determining metrics before and after the implementation of processes to conclude program effectiveness. Criterion-referenced instruments should be utilized in determining gains, comparing results to previous years (state/district/building/class), and evaluating teaching and learning methods, as well as materials. This leads to a quantifiable measure of performance in addition to enhanced quality of your end product—student achievement.

Keys to Implementation

Adaptive values and continual improvement efforts endure highs and lows, in addition to numerous potential challenges. We need to not only embrace change; we need to create it!

Fostering a culture of learning and tracking, with all teachers and staff understanding that their opinions are important and useful to the overall system, is only half the battle; in order to continually improve, we must *measure results after an intense implementation. This entire process will be an eye-opening experience for not just school leaders, but for the staff, students and parents alike. Because it is imperative to include all stakeholders and to explain expectations*

Beyond Theory

throughout implementation, your CIP will offer a great framework for changing the way you do business. Track where you were and compare where you are against where you want and/ or need to be. One successful comparative measurement practice involves a review of the following under Cylinder 8:

1. Proficiency changes
2. State achievement score trends
3. Subgroup achievement
4. State Assigned Building report card
5. District assessment results by school, grade level, teacher, and student
6. Learning gap by disaggregated group
7. Climate and culture changes

After absorbing the numbers, you should be prepared to begin reviewing and revising your CIP.

Using data, establish that continued growth is your focus, constantly monitor and measure results, make adjustments to lesson plans and execute your strategic plan for greater student achievement. This ongoing process supports the desire to respond quickly to results, and allows students to self-monitor, reflect, set goals, and take responsibility for their continual development.

Although measuring results and outcomes at various school levels may look differently based on the age of the students being served, the process is still necessary when determining successful implementation of the previous cylinders in meeting your needs.

Here is an example of some of the actual data from the Licking Heights Local Schools, Ohio.

Proficiency	2009–2010	2010–2011	% Gain
Reading	83.3%	90.9%	+ 7.6%
Writing	86.0%	96.2%	+ 9.8%
Mathematics	76.3%	84.8%	+ 8.5%
Social Studies	82.3%	93.8%	+ 11.5%
Science	67.2%	84.6%	+ 17.4%

Figure 17: 10th Grade Ohio Graduation Test, accessible through the State of Ohio Department of Education website under "Report Card Files."

Administration and staff members must work collaboratively: monitoring the right data, posing the right questions, and pinpointing probable solutions, for instant implementation. School success has a direct correlation to increasing expectations; buy-in from teachers, parents, and students; and, the demand for consistency by all involved in the improvement plan. Additionally, the monitoring and active involvement achieved from working Professional Learning Communities encourages teachers while creating a source of accountability that sets the tone for a positive school culture.

Here are several questions which guide collegial and student centered discussions during the school year, and again during the measurement of your year-end results.

- What information do students already know?
- What did students learn during the lesson based on evidence?
- What new information was learned during the lesson that was not planned?
- What will/did we pay attention to weekly/quarterly/each semester?
- What academic vocabulary is/was essential for the student's success on assessments?
- What changes in teaching practices need to take place based on the most recent formative evaluations?
- How do/did we provide feedback to students?
- How will/did students use feedback from the formative evaluations?
- What new teacher behaviors might have impacted student achievement?
- What do/did you attribute the student successes/challenges?
- What are/were the challenges to implementing and sustaining intervention efforts, and how will we combat them as a team?

When reviewing and revising your CIP it is important to compare apples to apples. Focus on the following:

- Proficiency results
- State achievement results
- Subgroup results
- Building report card
- District assessments
- Learning gaps found in disaggregated groups

Cathy's Commentary: Measuring Your Results and Celebrating Successes

Progress monitoring using an assessment schedule is critical if you are truly interested in changing your current reality and seeing great results. Without monitoring your progress you are stabbing in the dark every time you assess your students. In our north Florida secondary school, we developed a monitoring structure that allowed us to follow a simple cycle for assessment and tracking student learning. Teachers would always start by assessing for learning. This formative assessment provided a starting point for teaching and shaped the entire instructional process. Using the assessment data, teachers would present the concepts students needed, provide students an opportunity to apply the concept in real life situations, and then reassess to check for mastery of the concepts presented. This cycle would then help teachers plan for next steps, formulate new groups based on the level of student mastery, and customize the work based on student need.

This teaching and learning cycle was critical in our success. Teachers complained initially because they had difficulty understanding how they would be able to do this with the frequency needed to see real change without, quite frankly, working themselves to death. I could truly empathize; however, I was confident the results they would see would make their efforts worthwhile. I should tell you that we did monitor our students outside of the district's electronic system because we were doing more than the regularly scheduled district exams. Our system allowed us the flexibility of building in assessments that we needed to shift our instruction quickly and address specific concerns before unproductive practices became habit. It also provided a way to keep students engaged in self-reflection, tracking progress, and setting new short-term goals. We used student-tracking sheets in each of our student's folders so it was personal. Kids enjoyed the charting of their data and were thrilled when they could actually check off the standards they had mastered. Evaluating changes and growth offered both the teacher and the student an opportunity to experience success and to celebrate progress frequently which kept them motivated to continue to keep trying their best.

Once the teachers determined what data actually mattered and how much targeted instruction reduced their workload, our teachers and students learned the importance of spending time on data. In my Language Arts courses, for instance, the teachers worked collaboratively to develop assessments and used these common assignments and assessments as a method of normalizing their classrooms. Collaboratively they would review their results of formative assessments, determine the appropriate next steps based on those results, and then go back to implement their collective best practice(s). In this monitoring, they paid particular attention to subgroups measured specifically on the state assessment. Although they did not always find themselves in the same groups for instruction, students were grouped on the tracking forms for progress monitoring. The teachers would often speak of the pride students would experience when they were able to grasp a concept and move to enrichment or extension groups with kids they always considered to be "smart". Using data to shift students between groups also had a positive impact on many students' self-esteem and behavior. The classrooms became more collaborative because on any given day and based on any given subject, each kid could be the smart kid or in the smart kid group. The impact this had on the culture of the classroom and ultimately the school was unmatched.

Addressing the needs of students and responding to the data wasn't always easy and the picture wasn't always the best. In many instances, when performing a learning gap analysis, we would be troubled by the limited movement in some subgroups and would have to start to look at academic and non-academic factors that could be impacting student learning. Because of the make-up of our school we knew we had to look at factors we could control such as curriculum, teaching, strategies, classroom environment, supplemental materials, and structure. We were also clear that we had to somehow minimize the impact of the factors we had no control over at all. We looked, as a school, at things such as attendance, tardies, home structure or environment, exposure and use of external academic supports such as after-school programs or tutoring, and other non-academic factors and found ways to supplement as much as possible.

We developed strategies for improving attendance and held parents accountable for the role they played in their students' success or failure in our school. We developed an attendance intervention plan that involved contacting parents directly when kids missed 5 days of school and at various intervals thereafter. Let's just say this aggressive effort involved stages that included home visits and requiring parents to come into the school for attendance intervention meetings. Fortunately, our state also allowed us to report attendance issues to the state and parents could be arrested or have their driver's licenses suspended if their students were chronically absent or late. This made it easy for us to enforce our intervention steps and force compliance.

The processes we used to really dig deep into our students' abilities was both beneficial to the students and enlightening for our teachers. As a result of this very different kind of analysis, teacher-student relationships improved and a community of learners focusing only on success became our way of work. Our school family worked together to take away the excuses and we would not allow the students to use their circumstances as an excuse either. Once we acknowledged the problems, then we worked collaboratively to get back to the business at hand, mastering the standards.

In this school, while focusing on data specific teaching and learning, we were able to see tremendous success school-wide. The gains in reading proficiency were over 82% and our writing proficiency rate was the highest in the district for non-dedicated magnets. Our math gains were also great that year. Our lowest quartile gains were 62% greater than they had been in the past 3 years and our overall math proficiency rates increased by over 16%.

After reviewing our performance data, measuring our results, and celebrating our success we went into a process of developing new SMART goals and revising our continual improvement plan to address our new reality. The data team, teacher teams, and the administrative staff worked collaboratively to set new targets, revise our scheduling configurations, shifting teams of teachers based on their greatest point of impact or where they had the best results, and started to discuss kids and their needs one-by-one and name-by-name. We collaboratively worked on deciding next steps and the implementation cycle continued. Back to Cylinder 1.

Scott's Thoughts

Using data to make daily decisions about instruction . . . now that's what I'm talking about! For me, this is the most important of the eight cylinders. You may remember my opening story about my challenging meeting with my superintendent. My school had just experienced a significant drop in our performance numbers and I was facing the difficult task of finding a way to improve our achievement. That is when we started tracking data and using data to make daily decisions about instruction. That 34% proficient score in Communication Arts became a 74% score in that first year and consistently has been around the 80% proficient mark for a number of years. Our 56% score in math became an 81% proficient score in that first year in math. We started tracking our data. We started meeting on a regular basis and discussing each student in the building every single month. We began to create individualized plans to help each student achieve at a higher level based on their monthly assessment scores. The conversations were excellent! Not only were homeroom teachers discussing their students, but their colleagues were piping in with stories of best practices and how they had had similar students struggling with similar concepts and how they used certain strategies to help their students find success. What is more important than teachers collaborating with each other to help students learn? Each month when we came together as a grade-level team, we created "unofficial" IEP's to help all of our students achieve at a higher level. We were creating plans utilizing differentiated instruction to help our highest performing students right alongside with our lowest students.

Periodically, at grade-level meetings, we would invite Title I reading and math teachers, special education teachers, ELL teachers and other staff members who were a part of our students' daily instructional routine. This is what Professional Learning Communities are all about! Motivated staff members coming together, working together, collaborating together to create powerful learning plans to help our students gain in their knowledge.

When I speak at conferences or in schools/districts, I share the extreme importance of having a great deal of current data available to make positive decisions about instruction. In many schools, the only common data they possess is their state achievement data. It is VITAL to have common assessments, preferably every month, to give educators a clear snapshot of the progress being made in their classrooms and throughout their schools.

Using monthly data was one of the major keys in the success at Crestwood. Before we started using common assessments, we were never a Missouri Top 10 school. For the nine years we were using data analysis to drive our instruction, we were a Top 10 school each year. Accomplishing any task or meeting any goal for nine years in a row speaks to the importance of that school's or that organization's best practices. I tell you "data analysis" is definitely a best practice.

As the principal or leader, your participation in the data discussions is key. In many schools, the principals lead from behind their desks and don't have knowledge of individual students' strengths and weaknesses. Administrators need to get off of their seats, get out of their offices and be out in the hallways and classrooms. One of the key jobs for administrators is to be directly involved in these student discussions and have knowledge of the students in their buildings so they can be key contributors in the instructional conversations and not administrative by-standers.

As Schmoker states "The most obvious impediment to a results orientation is the failure at the beginning of the year to **put the data in front of the teachers**, have them look at it and then generate a manageable number of measurable goals based on the previous year's scores. That should be **job one** for administrators" (HOPE Foundation, 2002). Get the data out there and bring in your amazing teams—your grade-level teachers, reading and math instructors, special education, ELL, etc.—and create specific learning plans for your students. Cylinder 8 can have an amazing impact on the achievement in your schools. Use your data to improve your instruction and that improved instruction will impact the quality of your schoolhouse more than any other cylinder discussed thus far.

Beyond Theory . . . Where Did the Journey Lead?

Ty's Final Take

Since the long ride to the urban elementary school, Ty has been on an educational journey of continual improvement. The urban elementary school made academic gains in all grade levels; however, at one grade level the results resemble what Doug Reeves calls a 90/90/90 school. This is where 90 percent of the students are minority, 90 percent received free/reduced breakfast and lunch, and 90 percent are successful based on state assessments (Princeton City Schools Summer Institute, 2004). Who would have imagined a school with this composition to be successful academically?

Ty's departure from the urban elementary school took him to a suburban/urban junior high school outside Columbus, Ohio. The junior high school he led was designed for 700 students and housed roughly 1120 students. As you can imagine, an overcrowded building should create some challenges academically and behaviorally for administration and staff members. Administration and staff members working together on components of the reform effort, lead to high student achievement and growth for the junior high school according to Battelle for Kids data. In his journey within the school district, he was able to open a new junior high school. The new school relieved the older junior high school of roughly 620 students. He remained at the new junior high for another two years before his next mission.

This mission was a rural/urban high school in a neighboring school district that was one of the fastest growing school systems in the state. The district had grown over 39% in 10 years, along with a diverse population swelling to roughly 40% up from 10% during the same period! As you can imagine, this type of growth can provide many opportunities for administration and staff to use components of the reform. The first few opportunities that he and his staff addressed were improving test scores on the state's high school graduation test (OGT); decreasing disciplinary concerns to allow more teachable moments for staff within classrooms; and improving student ACT participation and test scores. Ty and his staff, through hard work, saw improvements in all of these areas based on national and state data.

Within the same district as the high school, Ty was promoted and provided the opportunity to take on the role of leading curriculum and instruction. He was charged to work with the district administrators in using components of the ECRM as a method to close the achievement gap and raise expectations for all students. He demonstrated success and is now a superintendent in Ohio where we would expect to see continued results.

Cathy's Silos to Systems Shift: The Team Is Still Making Strides

The positive changes in our school performance came primarily from the shifts in attitude and atmosphere developed through our new way of work. The model we implemented facilitated growth in our building and provided a sense of direction and a framework to guide our processes. The year following our drop in scores was one where it seemed the entire world was against us. Like any good family, we leaned on each other and agreed to implement our plan with fidelity. We focused only on moving our students and doing it by any means necessary. As a result, our scores soared. We had the highest gains in writing proficiency and our lowest quartile gains were tremendous. I could share more about the academic shifts but we feel it is necessary to also highlight the cultural shifts that occurred and how that impacted student performance.

The shift in adult practices became systemic and as teachers began to collaborate and use data as the basis for their instructional decisions the kids noticed and responded to the change. We created a data warehouse or "war room" and held PLC meetings in that area whenever a new data set was received and posted. Because we identified student groups and posted pictures along with other pertinent information on our high risk or high needs kids, it was not uncommon to hear teachers connecting to and supporting students they did not teach on a daily basis. Kids noticed adults knew them by name and could tell them what they needed to improve on or how they were progressing. Teachers, counselors, coaches, and staff all began to talk to their kids about their work and discuss expectations because it was no longer a secret or one person's task to complete. Everyone was able to address their students based on discussion in the PLCs and kids could feel the difference.

The level of rigor increased as teachers worked together to divide the work and produce a stronger product in the classroom. Students were provided opportunities to work at the level of expected performance, with support, until they were able to work at that level independently. Students and teachers learned to track their performance and work collaboratively to set goals for their own performance as well as for the performance of their students. For the first time, kids and teachers knew where they were as it related to performance targets and each knew what they needed to do to meet those targets when asked. The school was abuzz with positive talk and competition between teams to earn the highest gains on each school-wide or grade-level common assessment became the norm. Disciplinary incidents went down because teachers kept kids engaged and held them accountable for their work no matter what. Kids quickly learned that it was much easier to stay in class and cooperate than it was to make up work or potentially cause their team to suffer because they were in trouble. The conversations and constant focus on moving students transformed the school. The ECRM placed accountability factors front and center and provided a roadmap to success.

The kids and adults were rewarded for their hard work and the school was a much better place. We saw academic and nonacademic changes and the school was proud. Participation in activities and bridging the gap to the future became the norm for students who traditionally could not see beyond the school day. We added a band program, under the direction of Mr. Moses Evans, that outnumbered and outperformed many of the high school bands in the area. Prior to our shift, kids were not interested in nor were they provided the opportunity for such activities. Teachers were too tired to sponsor them and kids were not interested in taking part. Our kids were having fun and we were building pride both in our school and in our community. Our amazing middle school marching band won numerous competitions and after revamping our guidance department, making it more student centered, we were well on our way. We engaged our steadfast guidance counselor, Pat Warren, who worked tirelessly to build a social bridge to support and provide wraparound services to both the students and their families. She went on to be recognized as Counselor of the Year for the school district. I was thrilled with our progress. Our staff and our students had a lot to be proud of as well.

Scott Receives Another Phone Call

Remember our 34.5 percent communication arts score in 2004? And then in 2005 how it jumped to 73.6 percent? That year, on the same morning on the same date as the year before—August 16, at 8:15 a.m.—my phone rang once again, and my superintendent was on the line.

"Scott, do you have a minute?" he asked.

"Sure I do!" I responded.

"Come on over."

This time, the drive was a little more pleasant. For whatever reason, the six traffic lights between my school and central office were all green. I almost expected a doorman to greet me at the main lobby and open the door for me. As I settled in to the superintendent's office, once again the topic of discussion was Crestwood's student achievement. For the first time during my three-year tenure, Crestwood had the highest achievement in the district in math and communication arts. My superintendent was very pleased and I was so glad that all of our hard work with the eight cylinders had improved our achievement. However, as I mentioned earlier, my superintendent had a keen way of continuing to motivate me to do my best work. After he shared his praise for Crestwood, he did not allow me to leave without making sure I would remain focused on continual improvement in the years to come.

"So tell me, Scott, which of these years—2003–04 or 2004–05—accurately depict your leadership?" he said toward the end of our meeting. "Is it 2004 with your low scores, or 2005 with your high scores? I hope that 2005 wasn't a fluke!"

I shared with my superintendent the reasons for our growth in 2004–05, including the great work accomplished by our building committees and the focus on data, which allowed for our student achievement to improve. All year long, our staff continued to do all they could to keep Crestwood on the path toward continual school improvement and high achievement.

So the story of two phone calls . . . and in between how the ECRM impacted our school. It is powerful that in each of the nine years since I received that first phone call that we were a Missouri Top Ten School, as well as a Missouri Gold Star School, a State and National School of Character, and a National Blue Ribbon School. Focusing on each of these eight cylinders created a culture in our school where every student was successful due to the incredibly talented and caring staff members who worked with these students. What did our data say? The Eight Cylinder Reform Model for improving student achievement worked and worked very well!

Scott retired in 2013 and is currently working as a motivational speaker and consultant. After sixteen years as a teacher and sixteen years as a principal, Scott misses the daily contact with children but enjoys his role helping numerous schools improve their achievement. Scott and his wife Becky, who recently retired, are enjoying some travel opportunities and spending more time with their family. They have more grandchildren on the way and are very excited about their new additions to their family.

References

Armstrong, T. (2006). *The best schools: how human development research should inform educational practice.* Alexandria, Va.: Association for Supervision and Curriculum Development.

Barth, R. S. (2001). *Learning by heart.* San Francisco: Jossey-Bass.

BenShea, N. (2002). *Great quotes to inspire great teachers.* Thousand Oaks, Calif.: Corwin Press.

Blankstein, A. M. (2004). *Failure is not an option: six principles that guide student achievement in high-performing schools.* Thousand Oaks, Calif.: Corwin Press.

Blankstein, A. M. (2010). *Failure is not an option: 6 principles for making student success the only option.* Thousand Oaks, Calif.: Corwin Press.

Blase, J.L., & Kirby, P.C. (1992, December). The power of praise: a strategy for effective principals. NAASP Bulletin, 76(548), 69-77

Caine, R. N., & Caine, G. (1997a). *Education on the edge of possibility.* Alexandria, VA: Association of Supervision and Curriculum Development.

Canfield, J., & Hansen, M. V. (1993). *Chicken soup for the soul: 101 stories to open the heart & rekindle the spirit.* Deerfield Beach, FL: Health Communications.

Casals, P., & Kahn, A. E. (1981). *Joys and sorrows: his own story.* London: Eel Pie Pub.

Jim Collins (2001). *Good to great.* New York: Harper Business

Cottrell, David (2002). *Monday morning leadership. 8 mentoring sessions you can't afford to miss.* Dallas, Texas: CornerStone Leadership Institute.

Cottrell, D., & Reed, D. (2004). *Monday morning customer service.* Dallas, Tex.: CornerStone Leadership Institute.

Covey, S. M., & Merrill, R. R. (2006). *The speed of trust: the one thing that changes everything.* New York: Free Press.

Covey, S. R. (1989). *The seven habits of highly effective people: restoring the character ethic.* New York: Simon and Schuster.

Csikszentmihalyi, M. (1990). *Flow: the psychology of optimal experience.* New York: Harper & Row.

Darling-Hammond, L. (1997). *The right to learn: a blueprint for creating schools that work.* San Francisco: Jossey-Bass.

DeBruyn, Robert (2002). *Understanding and relating to parents.* Kansas: The Master Teacher, Inc.

Deming, W. Edwards (1986). *Out of the crisis.* MIT Press.

DuFour, R. (2004). *Whatever it takes: how professional learning communities respond when kids don't learn.* Bloomington, Ind.: National Educational Service.

DuFour, R. (2004, May). "What is a 'professional learning community'?" *Educational Leadership.* 63(8), 6-11.

DuFour, R., & Eaker, R. E. (1998). *Professional learning communities at work: best practices for enhancing student achievement.* Bloomington, Ind.: National Education Service.

DuFour, R., Eaker, R. E., & DuFour, R. B. (2005). *On common ground: the power of professional learning communities.* Bloomington, Ind.: National Educational Service.

Edmonds, R. (1986). Characteristics of effective schools. In *The School Achievement of Minority Children: New Perspectives,* edited by U. Neisser. Hillsdale, N.J.: Lawrence Erlbaum

References

Englert, R. M. (1993). *Understanding the urban context and conditions of practice of school administration*. Philadelphia, PA: National Center on Education in the Inner Cities.

Fox, J. E., & Certo, J. (1999) *Recruiting and retaining teachers: a review of the literature*, Richmond, VA: Metropolitan Educational Research Consortium

Fullan, M. (2001). *Leading in a culture of change*. San Francisco: Jossey-Bass.

Fullan, M., & Hargreaves, A. (1996). *What's worth fighting for in your school?* New York: Teachers College Press.

Fullan, M., Stiegelbauer, S. M., & Fullan, M. (1991). *The new meaning of educational change*. Toronto: Ontario Institute for Studies in Education.

Glatthorn, A. A., Jones, B. K., & Adams, B. A. (2006). *Developing highly qualified teachers: a handbook for school leaders*. Thousand Oaks, CA: Corwin Press.

Gregory, G., & Chapman, C. (2002). *Differentiated instructional strategies: one size doesn't fit all*. Thousand Oaks, Calif.: Corwin Press.

Hall, G. and Hord, S. (2001). *Implementing change: patterns, principles, and potholes*. Boston, MA: Allyn and Bacon.

Hargreaves, A., & Fullan, M. (1998). *What's worth fighting for out there?* New York: Teachers College Press.

HOPE Foundation. (2002). *Failure is not an option: how high-achieving schools succeed with all students* (Video Series). United States. Corwin Press.

Kozol, J. (2005). *The shame of the nation: the restoration of apartheid schooling in America*. New York: Crown.

Killion, J. & Roy, P. (2009) *Becoming a learning school*. National Staff Development Council

Lortie, D. C. (1975). *School teacher: a sociological study.* Chicago: University of Chicago Press.

Marzano, R. J. (2003). *What works in schools: translating research into action.* Alexandria, Va.: Association for Supervision and Curriculum Development.

Marzano, R. J. (2007). *The art and science of teaching: a comprehensive framework for effective instruction.* Alexandria, Va.: Association for Supervision and Curriculum Development.

Marzano, R.J., Pickering, D., & Pollock, J. (2001). *Classroom instruction that works: research-based strategies for increasing student achievement.* Alexandria, VA: Association of Supervision and Curriculum Development.

Marzano, R. J., Waters, T., & McNulty, B. A. (2005). *School leadership that works: from research to results.* Alexandria, Va.: Association for Supervision and Curriculum Development.

NEA Foundation, (2000). *Engaging public support for teachers' professional development overview.*

Nelson, B. (1994). *1001 ways to reward employees.* New York: Workman Pub.

Peters, S. G. (2008). *Teaching to capture and inspire all learners: bringing your best stuff every day!* Thousand Oaks, CA: Corwin Press.

Pollock, J. E. (2007). *Improving student learning one teacher at a time.* Alexandria, Va.: Association for Supervision and Curriculum Development.

Reed, D. & Cottrell, D. (2004). *Monday morning customer service.* Dallas, TX: Cornerstone Leadership Institute.

References

Richardson, J. (1999, September). High poverty doesn't have to mean low performance. *RESULTS Newsletter National Staff Development Council*, p.4

Schmoker, M. J. (1996). *Results: the key to continuous school improvement*. Alexandria, Va.: Association for Supervision and Curriculum Development.

Schmoker, M. J. (2001). *The results fieldbook: practical strategies from dramatically improved schools*. Alexandria, Va.: Association for Supervision and Curriculum Development.

Schmoker, M. J. (2006). *Results now: how we can achieve unprecedented improvements in teaching and learning*. Alexandria, Va.: Association for Supervision and Curriculum Development.

Simmons, A. (2000). *Guide to today's teacher recruitment challenges*. Belmont, MA: Recruiting New Teachers.

Smith, W. F., & Andrews, R. L. (1989). *Instructional leadership: how principals make a difference*. Alexandria, Va.: Association for Supervision and Curriculum Development.

Stiggins, R. J. (1994). *Student-centered classroom assessment*. New York: Merrill.

Thernstrom, A. M., & Thernstrom, S. (2003). *No excuses: closing the racial gap in learning*. New York: Simon & Schuster.

Whitaker, T. (2003). *What great principals do differently: fifteen things that matter most*. Larchmont, N.Y.: Eye on Education.

Wiggins, G. & McTighe, J. (2005). *Understanding by design* (Expanded 2nd Ed. USA). Alexandria, Va.: Association for Supervision and Curriculum Development.

Williams, B. (2003). *Closing the achievement gap: a vision for changing beliefs and practices*. Alexandria, Va.: Association for Supervision and Curriculum Development.

Zmuda, A., Kuklis, R., & Kline, E. (2004). *Transforming schools: creating a culture of continuous improvement*. Alexandria, VA: Association for Supervision and Curriculum Development.